Diplomat
IN THE KITCHEN
by Jeremiah Knight

DIPLOMAT IN THE KITCHEN

JEREMIAH KNIGHT

Washington, 2024

DEDICATION

In Memory of Gussie Mae Knight

1916-2019

When I was five years old, I started my culinary journey by helping my mother cook at home. I vividly remember my line-chef duties of mixing, stirring, and beating, so the recipes could come together. Mom said I was too young to use a knife to chop, and I couldn't get too close to the stove. Little did she know that when I visited Grandma's home, it was a different story. Sure, I did the mixing and stirring, but Grandma also had me cutting, frying, and doing all sorts of things! I felt powerful and creative, turning wholesome foods into masterpieces, with Grandma by my side. My time with her in the kitchen wasn't just about cooking lessons; it was full of life lessons.

Over piles of flour and bowls of cracked eggs, Grandma shared memories of our family history. I even learned that some of the recipes we made together were dishes she picked up while working in the houses of "white folks." Her backyard was as beautiful and bountiful as her spirit. She was a true steward of the land. She and my Granddad (who must have thought he was still living in rural Jamaica) created a vast garden where fresh veggies, herbs, and tons of fruit grew everywhere. Unknowingly, I had been practicing "farm to table" since I was a child, creating meals with her that were enjoyed by granddad and the rest of my family. I distinctly remember spending summer afternoons canning peaches with her. We made some of the best peach cobbler in the world. Autumn was always enchanting. We'd harvest apples, picked with love, from her four trees. They, like my Grandma, were always the sweetest.

My Grandmother was never afraid to experiment in the kitchen, often trying something many times until she got it just right. Her taste for adventure took her around most of the United States, packing her grandchildren and children of her church members along for the journey to attend church conventions. I guess that's where my adventurous spirit in the kitchen and as a globetrotter comes from. She even made trips to visit me abroad, as I worked in U.S. embassies.

As the years passed, she eventually turned her kitchen over to me. Our roles reversed; she would chop, stir, and clean as I created three meals a day for her and my granddad, as often as I could. She gave me space to experiment and share what I learned from my travels. Most of all, she made me remember, time and time again, how everything somehow tasted better when made in her kitchen. From the poultry to the pots, everything there was soaked in her love.

When I began this journey of **Diplomat in the Kitchen**, I envisioned my Grandmother being a part of the celebration. Well, God had other plans. So now, she's looking down from heaven, enjoying it all the same. There is no one I would want to dedicate this book to, other than the one person who played so many roles in my life. She was my Grandma, Second Mom, First and Always Pastor (yet never preachy), and most of all, My Very Best Friend. **She was my Living Angel!**

When she suddenly passed, while I was in the process of planning her birthday, I thought I couldn't continue with this book. I often got upset with God, because I thought it was unfair that he made me love her so much; God knew I would have to spend a large portion of my life without her in it. It took me months to start writing again. But, I knew deep down, she would have been extremely disappointed with me if I had not finished it! So, Grandma, you will not only live on in my thoughts and my heart, but also within the pages of this book. People around the world will learn of your sainted soul! **I adore you forever my love!**

THANKS!

Creating **Diplomat in the Kitchen** provided me with the opportunity to enrich old friendships and foster new ones to help this book become a reality. From words of encouragement, advice, recipe suggestions, your input was key to the book's success. However, in particular I would like to thank Aliya Ewing for your job as principal editor. You transformed my ideas into art! Thanks to Moya Thomas for your role as secondary editor (recipes). What can I say about Yanolis Espinosa, Keyla Diaz and Elyoenay Tejada!? You all formed the best team anyone could imagine having to help me make this project into a reality. To Mike Levine who shared an extra eye of editing to the final version. In memory of Maria Rosa Peralta Diaz whose dishes and plates were used throughout this book. And finally to my dear friend Elmira Web for helping to put the final touches on organizing the journey.

Illustration: Jas Knight

CREDITS

ISBN: 979-8-218-51836-3

Editors: Aliya Ewing | Moya Thomas | Mike Levine

Proofreaders: Keyla Diaz Peralta | Yanoli Espinosa

Front Cover photo by Hector Mirabal

Photography: Hector Mirabal, Chewy Lin, 123fr, Adobe stock

Food Stylist: Andrea Garzon

Illustrations and design by Elyoenay Tejada

Charcoal Illustration: Jas Knight

Publisher: Catalyst Press Books

Consortium Book Sales & Distribution, The Keg House 34 13th Avenue NE, Suite 101, Minneapolis, MN 55413-1007

First 500 edition 2025

PROLOGUE

The first thing I want to say about the author of this remarkable work is that Jeremiah is an exceptional host. His recipes are imbued with a profound connection to every individual he welcomes to his table. Jeremiah is a masterful storyteller, weaving narratives that transport you to unexpected places with each delectable bite, enriching the dining experience. Your soul soars as it engages with the adventures of this audacious diplomat.

Jeremiah's free spirit has led him to a myriad of experiences, each adding a unique flavor to his culinary expertise. Those of us fortunate enough to sit at his table benefit greatly from his rich tapestry of life. We share a mutual appreciation for our global pantry, dreaming without bounds, and reveling in the joy of sharing, cooking, and connecting through the vibrant spectrum of flavors. This common ground has forged a deep friendship, and I must confess that knowing Jeremiah has often been a source of inspiration.

Our long conversations began when he resided in South Sudan. Perhaps feeling the pangs of solitude, he welcomed my eager curiosity about the local culture each evening. Then, almost seamlessly, he transitioned to a more tropical yet equally enigmatic locale—the Marshall Islands. His days became more colorful, his stories more vivid, reflecting the dynamic cultures he immersed himself in. Here was a place many dream of visiting, and Jeremiah thrived, sharing and living these cultures, all while upholding his duties as a distinguished diplomat representing his country with honor.

Unforgettable are the grand Thanksgiving feasts celebrated with open doors, where an immense table brims with comforting, homely dishes, showcasing the richness and diversity of American culture. This cookbook is not merely a collection of recipes; it is an invitation to Jeremiah's table, offering a glimpse into his story and equipping you to become a gracious host. From the perspective of a humble yet adventurous soul who explores the world through its flavors and its people, this book is your passport to culinary excellence.

Catherine Lemoine
Chef

Yanoli Espinosa, Jeremiah Knight and Catherine Lemoine

INTRODUCTION

"Diplomat in the Kitchen: Culinary adventures one recipe at a time."

Isn't it amazing how smell and taste can transport you to a time and place? The scent of fresh baked bread may bring warm childhood memories of Grandma's kitchen; the spicy kick of scotch bonnet pepper might take you to the beach shores of Jamaica, a plate of jerk chicken in hand, enjoying the perfect sunset with your best friends; this is the power of food! History, culture, and language season every dish created. Across the ages, people have shared their culture via culinary tradition. Food provides a perfect platform for exchange, creativity, and strengthening relationships.

Cooking and creating a journey through food are in the DNA of my family. From my grandparents who co-owned two family restaurants, to my uncle who was a master chef in London, to my aunt's Jamaican eatery in the center of Decatur, Georgia, food has been at the heart of our souls. I'm happiest when I see people enjoying a meal that I've created. I love to see them gleefully stuffed; my late Uncle David was the one who passed that passion on to me! This proud Jamaican would cook some of the best yard food (traditional Jamaican cuisine) and then go on to playfully force people to eat until they could only lay on the floor in bliss. At that point you would see a big smile on Uncle David's face. I am just the same. I love to see every bit of the food devoured and people sitting uncomfortably on a sofa, belt buckles ready to be loosened a notch. Even better, I love when they ask me, "Do you mind if I take a nap in the guestroom?" That means I fed them particularly well.

Coupling good food with good conversation (or a good nap!) is also something I learned from my parents and grandparents, I can vividly remember their homes being the places to be for Sunday dinners and holidays, the height of comfort and exchange. There was never a moment growing up when my home wasn't filled with aromas emanating from the kitchen and guests continually coming over to partake with us. To this day, I would rather have a home smell like freshly baked cinnamon rolls, a pot bubbling with curried chicken, or sorrel simmering, than the commercial candle scents of flowers and fresh linen. So, as I began traveling the world, it came as no surprise that the first aspect of culture I wanted to experience in each country was its gastronomy: the communion of food preparation and culture, the study of regional cooking styles, and overall, the art of eating well and living even better.

Diplomat in the Kitchen is my personal gastronomic memoir of my journeys across the globe. As an American diplomat, I've had the pleasure of dining with strangers-turned-life-long-friends; I've sat at restaurant tables from Argentina to Istanbul, and each excursion has come with its own story. As you travel through this memoir, you'll find that I often share my personal take on a traditional recipe. This is by no means an attempt to disregard the culinary legacies of individual cultures, but rather to celebrate global flavors and the concept of food as a vehic*le to bridge culture*s. For this, in the culinary world (and in your home kitchens) I hope I'm given diplomatic immunity.

I believe the kitchen should be a safe place where people can gather and share, regardless of their background, to create an experience that not only satisfies taste buds, but also serves as the welcome committee to global cultural heritage. There is definitely merit in sticking to a strict definition of a particular dish or recipe (which you will also find throughout the book). However, in this global community which we live in, I believe we strengthen our ties when we bring a fusion of backgrounds and flavors into the conversation, then share in an inclusive and inviting way. This is what culinary diplomacy is all about! So I encourage you to use your own journey for inspiration as you travel through this book and add your own flair to the recipes I share. Think of each recipe as a passport stamp allowing entry into a new land; have fun with your exploration!

If you are like me, then you know traveling is always more fun when you have someone to experience it with. You'll find that in **Diplomat in the Kitchen**, I invite some friends to join me on this global excursion. Their added stories and recipes are perfect complements to my journey. Even though I've had the pleasure of traveling extensively, culinary journeys are not only for those who have money to globetrot. **Diplomat in the Kitchen** transforms every kitchen into a gateway to world travel simply by going to your neighborhood supermarket, or backyard garden, and harvesting the bounty, to create these taste-bud adventures.

Now grab your passport and let's get ready to travel!

TABLE OF CONTENTS

Photography: Chewy Lin

AFRIC

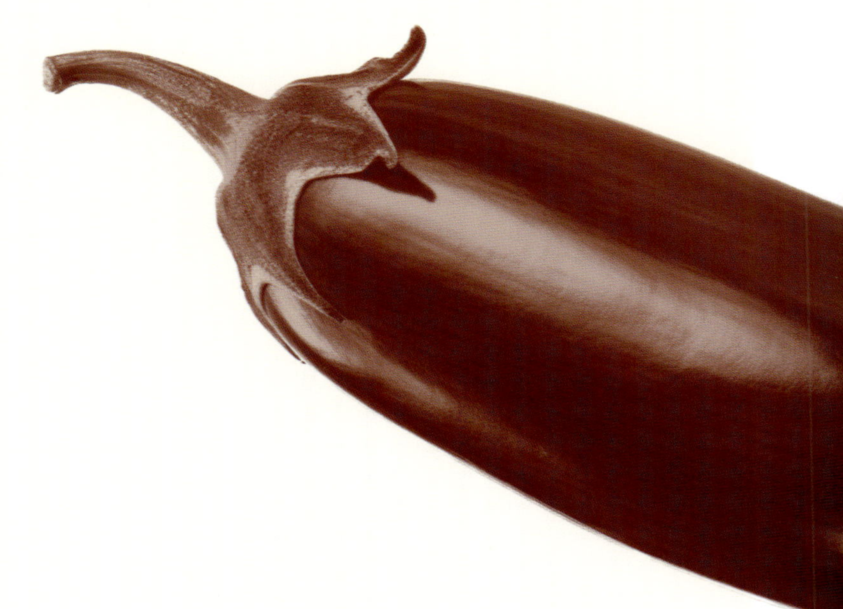

TUNISIA | MOROCCO | ALGERIA | EGYPT | SOUTH AFRICA | SOUTH SUDAN

TUNISIA

Exhausted after three flights and God knows how many hours in the air, I stepped on African soil for the first time in Tunis, Tunisia, 2003. During my 10 weeks interning at the U.S. Embassy, I explored the historic Roman ruins of Carthage and El Djem, the pristine beaches of Hammamet, and the enchanted deserts of the south. It was an unbelievable summer which not only solidified my desire to work as a diplomat, but also opened my taste buds to a world of new flavor adventures.

Tunisia's unique position as a crossroads of Africa, the Middle East, and Europe results in a cuisine that has been slowly simmered in rich history. Tunisian food is a hybrid of Mediterranean and desert dwellers' (native Berber) culinary traditions along with European influences. Over its history, the country has been ruled by the Phoenicians, Romans, Arabs, Turks, and French, each bringing its own flavor. As you walk the streets of Tunis, you can see from its architecture, people, and of course food that the land has served throughout time as a meeting point for various cultures. Its mosques, synagogues, and churches also paint a picture of religious diversity. And the best part for me was that most Tunisians are not bashful about sharing their culture, history, and of course food! Their love for all things spicy made the cuisine an instant hit with my palate. Like those of their North African neighbors, Tunisian dishes are cooked with vibrant spices like aniseed, mint, cumin, cilantro, cinnamon, and saffron. *Harissa* and fresh garlic paste are common condiments, while orange blossom and rose water are often used in desserts, giving a distinct floral profile to sweets.

I noticed upon arrival that there were no American fast-food chains. It wasn't that I was craving fast food; but it was my first experience being in a country that didn't have it as an option. Most would say that's a good thing, but after spending all day traveling, I would have welcomed being able to grab something quick. After a few days living in Tunis, I finally asked what people ate for "fast food": *shawarmas* were the answer.

You see, *shawarmas* are found throughout North Africa and the Middle East as a quick fix for the hungry soul. Particularly in Tunisia, with no western options for burgers and pizza, *shawarmas* are a go-to option for locals and foreigners alike.

Every chance I got I'd wander through the spice market section of Tunis' Medina, eating *shawarma* made fresh from street vendors. I took the advice of one of my local friends, and first ordered the chicken one s*tuffed with French fries*, spiced up with *Harissa* sauce! It was a gift from heaven, comforting, familiar, and yet new. From then on when I was hungry and didn't have time to cook, I would go down the street from my home and get a *shawarma*!

CHICKEN SHAWARMA

PREP
1 hour

COOK
35-40 mins.

SKILL LEVEL
Medium

SERVES
5-6

INGREDIENTS

Chicken seasoning:
- 2 lb. boneless skinless chicken thighs
- 2 lemons (juice)
- ⅓ cup olive oil
- 6 cloves garlic minced
- 2 tsp. sea salt
- 2 tsp. freshly ground black pepper
- 2 tsp. ground cumin
- 2 tsp. smoked paprika
- ½ tsp. turmeric
- 2 tsp. ground cinnamon
- 1-2 tsp. chili flakes, to taste
- 1 large yellow onion, peeled and quartered
- 2 tbsp. fresh chopped parsley

White Sauce:
- ½ cup plain yogurt
- 4 cloves roasted garlic, minced
- 2 tbsp. olive oil
- 1 tsp. white pepper

Additions:
- 1 medium cucumber
- 2 ripe tomatoes

INSTRUCTIONS

To make the marinade, combine lemon juice, olive oil, garlic, salt, pepper, cumin, paprika, turmeric, cinnamon, and red pepper flakes in a large bowl and whisk. Add the chicken thighs and onions. Cover and let it rest in the refrigerator for at least 24 hours.

Preheat the oven to 400° F.

Put chicken and onions in a deep roasting pan with a wire rack.

Place the pan in the middle of the oven and roast until the chicken is nice and brown and a little crispy. This should take 35-40 mins.

While the chicken is cooking, you can begin making the sauce. In a blender, combine the yogurt with the olive oil and already-roasted garlic cloves (you can roast these some hours ahead of time). Add in the white pepper and place in the refrigerator.

Remove the chicken and onion from the oven and let rest for 2 minutes. Place the chicken pieces on a chopping board and cut into small strips. Place the strips in a very hot frying pan with olive oil to make them a bit crispier.

Spread white sauce on a warmed pita bread (add hot sauce if desired) and then place chicken, parsley and onions inside along with the cucumbers and tomato slices.

To finish it how I had it in Tunisia, you can add some French fries!

TUNISIAN TAJINE

PREP
10 mins.

COOK
25-30 mins.

SKILL LEVEL
Easy

SERVES
6

AFRICA

Apparently, *shawarmas*, particularly the French fries-stuffed chicken ones I was hooked on, were frowned upon as incomplete meals. Luckily, my office was filled with wonderful Tunisian women who believed it was their mission to take care of me while interning. One of their self-imposed responsibilities was to ensure that I had an adequate Tunisian lunch – who was I to refuse? I took full advantage of every invitation to eat at the homes of my Tunisian friends, or have their kitchens come to me by way of the office lunch table.

As much as I love street vendor *shawarmas*, the whole "rushed" experience leaves something to be desired. People buy street food around the world because it's convenient when on-the-go. And oftentimes, you shovel the food in just as fast as it was purchased. That has its time and place (like when staggering off a 14-hour flight), but usually I love to sit down and savor the entire experience, appreciate what I am eating and who I'm enjoying it with. I love street food for its authentic qualities but at times I'd rather an equally authentic sit-down home cooked meal.

One of the dishes served at practically every social function I attended was the Tunisian Tajine. Unlike its culinary cousins in Morocco and Algeria (which use a special clay pot to stew meats and vegetables), the Tunisian version is what I would call North Africa's response to a frittata. It's simple but extremely tasty. It's often served as part of a breakfast meal, but also at lunch, or even at evening receptions and cocktails. As versatile as this dish is, I believe it should be incorporated into the culinary repertoire of every *Diplomat in the Kitchen*! Take a look at my take on this classic Tunisian dish.

INGREDIENTS

- **2 lb. boneless skinless chicken thighs**
- **1 lb. chicken or lamb, cut into small cubes about ¼ inch in size**
- **1 cup potatoes, peeled and chopped into ¼ inch cubes**
- **2 tbsp. tabil (see instruction on next page)**
- **¼ cup virgin olive oil**
- **small amount of water**
- **1 tsp. tomato paste**
- **a pinch salt (to taste)**
- **1 bunch parsley, finely chopped**
- **8 large eggs**
- **⅓ cup breadcrumbs**
- **¼ cup parmesan cheese**
- **¼ cup Romano cheese**

INSTRUCTIONS

Preheat your oven to 300° F.

Using a mortar and pestle, mash together your garlic and tabil mixture with a pinch of sea salt.

In a small saucepan, heat oil and then add garlic/tabil mixture. Stir for about 2-3 minutes. Add chicken and salt, then cook until browned. Finally, add tomato paste with a little water and cook for an additional 3-4 minutes.

Reduce heat and allow chicken to simmer until fully cooked. Set it aside and let it cool.

In a small frying pan, fry your potatoes until just very lightly brown.

In a large bowl, whisk eggs. Add parsley, potatoes, Romano cheese, breadcrumbs, and the chicken mixture then gently fold all the ingredients together. The consistency should be that of a quiche mixture (spongy and moist).

Salt to taste.

Pour your mixture into a baking dish. Bake for 30-50 minutes or until the center has set and the edges are golden brown.

TABIL SPICE BLEND

Tabil is a spice used widely throughout North Africa. It is often used on grilled meats, stews, and even salads. There are various methods of making it, but all versions include the majority of spices listed below. Store it and use it for later!

PREP	COOK	SKILL LEVEL	SERVES
10 mins.	2-5 mins.	Easy	6

INGREDIENTS

- 2 tbsp. coriander seeds
- 2 tsp. caraway seeds
- ½ tsp. fennel seeds
- ½ tsp. chili powder
- ½ tsp. black peppercorns
- ¼ tsp. cumin seeds
- ¼ tsp. turmeric powder
- ½ tsp. whole cloves
- 3 green or black cardamom pods
- ½ tsp. garlic powder

INSTRUCTIONS

Mix all spices except garlic powder in a heavy skillet.

Heat and stir continuously until you begin to smell the aromas (around 2-3 minutes at high heat).

Remove from heat and let cool.

Add garlic powder.

With a mortar and pestle, grind ingredients until they become a fine powder.

Store mixture in an airtight container.

TUNISIAN CUCUMBER SALAD

PREP	COOK	SKILL LEVEL	SERVES
10 mins.	0	Easy	4-5

INGREDIENTS

- 4-6 medium size tomatoes
- ½ a large red onion
- 1 cucumber
- ¼ cup chopped fresh parsley
- ¼ cup chopped fresh mint
- 2 tbsp. lemon juice
- 1 tsp. white vinegar
- 2 tbsp. olive oil
- salt and pepper to taste
- a sprinkling of whole olives

INSTRUCTIONS

Dice tomatoes, cucumber, and onion.

Add the vinegar, oil, lemon juice, salt, pepper, and mix well.

Add herbs and olives. Mix lightly.

Serve with a fresh baguette and butter!

MOROCCO

My dear friend Halima introduced me to *kefta* tagine. She and I met in 2006 while I was living in Santiago, Chile. Halima, being from Morocco, bonded with me over our mutual love for North Africa and my time spent living in Tunisia. Halima wasn't impressed with my stories of having "lived in North Africa" though. To her, no trip to the region is complete without experiencing the colorful flavors of her beloved Moroccan homeland, which she calls the "heart of North Africa and its cuisine." While I'm sure my Tunisian friends might disagree with that last part, she still has a valid point about global travel: exploring extensively within a region gives a fuller picture of the overall culture. Fast forward about ten years and our paths crossed again in Kingston, Jamaica. Her husband was leading the U.S. Embassy and I was one of his section heads. Halima and I often spoke about picking a date to cook together, when she would show me how to make some Moroccan dishes. However, our schedules always seemed to clash. One day while in her husband's office, he told me that I was being ordered to go to their home the following day at about noon to cook with Halima. I took this task from my boss seriously and promised to leave him some food (if we didn't eat all of it)! Upon entering the home, I shouted in a very sarcastic voice, "Finally I am going to learn how to cook North African food!" I was greeted by a big hug and laugh from Halima.

As Halima began to prepare her dish, she shared that as a child she would often take the six-hour drive from Rabat to the town of Nador to visit her grandmother, Zahara. Upon arrival, her dear grandmother would always have piping-hot *kefta* tagine waiting to welcome Halima and her family. The traditional meatball dish was always served to her with olives and washed down with a cup of mint tea. The dish evokes strong memories of deep-rooted family traditions. So, when I asked Halima what Moroccan food should be included in this book, she insisted that it be *kefta* tagine! She told me that this dish is the quick "go-to" meal when an unexpected visitor arrives, and you need to serve them something satisfying. *Kefta* tagine is also served as a lunch course.

During my cooking session with Halima, I began to understand just how much food plays a vital role in Moroccan society, and in ways that mirrored my own life, thousands of miles away. People would randomly pop up at my home, and my mom would always have something delicious to offer them, along with her warm smile. My grandmother did the same, as I'm sure her grandmother did too. It doesn't require a lot of effort to make someone feel welcome in your home, but the effects of your kind gestures are long-lasting. Simple dishes go a long way in showing your appreciation to visitors, and it's a great idea to have a tried-and-true dish that you can easily whip up at a moment's notice. I never look at it as an inconvenience, but rather an opportunity to make memories!

HALIMA'S KEFTA TAGINE

PREP
10 mins.

COOK
25-30 mins.

SKILL LEVEL
Easy

SERVES
6

INGREDIENTS

- ½ lb. ground beef (you can substitute ground lamb, turkey or chicken)
- 2 medium white onions
- 3-4 garlic cloves
- 2 large tomatoes
- 1 bunch fresh cilantro
- 1 tsp. crushed red pepper
- 4 tsp. ground cumin
- 2 tsp. black pepper
- 3 tsp. paprika
- 2 tsp. ground ginger
- 1 bay leaf
- ¼ cup tomato paste
- 4 tbsp. olive oil
- 4 tsp. sea salt
- ¼ cup chicken broth
- 2 eggs (optional)

AFRICA

INSTRUCTIONS

Peel, seed, and finely chop the tomatoes. Set aside.

In a deep skillet, saute half the quantity of onions along with the garlic in olive oil for approximately 5 minutes.

Add tomatoes, bay leaf, half the quantity of spices and chopped cilantro to skillet. Add tomato paste and simmer on low heat for about 10-15 minutes.

Combine the ground meat with the remainder of the spices, onions, garlic and cilantro, leaving enough cilantro for a garnish.

Use your hands to knead and create meatballs that are approximately 1 inch in diameter.

Add the meatballs to the tomato sauce along with ¼ cup of chicken broth—and cover.

Cook for about 30 to 40 minutes, or until the sauce is thick.

Cover and cook for an additional 7 to 10 minutes, or until the egg whites are solid and the yolks are only partially set.

Garnish with cilantro and serve immediately with slices of a baguette.

If adding egg, cover and cook for an additional 7-10 minutes.

Chef's tip: Make sure you roll the meatballs nice and small as instructed. You don't want large ones. The smaller the better. I would suggest serving it with chilled mint tea with lime, just as Halima's grandmother would.

MOROCCAN MAAKOUDA

PREP
35 mins.

COOK
0

SKILL LEVEL
Medium

SERVES
15

This is an excellent appetizer for any meal, especially those which would focus on the African continent or France.

INGREDIENTS

- 1 lb. peeled and boiled potatoes
- 2 tbsp. finely chopped parsley
- 1 clove garlic (finely chopped)
- 1 tbsp. chopped chives
- ½ tsp. sea salt
- ¼ tsp. ground black pepper

Dipping Batter:

- 1 tsp. dried yeast
- 1½ cup all-purpose flour
- ½ tsp. turmeric
- ½ tsp. salt
- 1 cup of milk
- 2½ to 3 cups oil for deep frying

INSTRUCTIONS

In a large bowl mash the potatoes until smooth and stir in the rest of the ingredients.

Activate the dry yeast by adding 2 tablespoons of lukewarm water in a small bowl. Mix and set aside for 6-8 minutes. Shape mashed potatoes into flattened circles, about 2 inches in diameter. Place in the refrigerator until ready to fry.

Once yeast is foaming, mix all ingredients and leave to rise for 30 minutes.

Depending on the flour you use, you can add a few tablespoons of water so the batter is not too thick. It should be light but not runny, otherwise it will break up during frying.

Heat oil until it 350⁰ F. I often toss a crushed clove of garlic until golden brown to gauge if oil is hot enough and adds seasoning.

Place battered potato cakes in hot oil and cook until golden brown (about 3 minutes).

Once ready, use a slotted spoon to transfer to a paper towel lined plate. Serve with *harissa* (a spicy North African sauce), or a simple puree of tomatoes, garlic, crushed hot peppers and salt.

ALMOND SMOOTHIE

PREP
5 mins.

COOK
0

SKILL LEVEL
Easy

SERVES
2 cups

INGREDIENTS

- ½ ripe avocado
- 1 cup almond milk
- ½ tsp. of almond flavoring
- 2 tsp. brown sugar or honey

INSTRUCTIONS

Mix all ingredients in a blender and top with shaved almonds.

SOUTH SUDAN

As the plane lowered over the capital city of Juba, South Sudan, I'll never forget the mixed emotions that overcame me. *Excited* to have the opportunity to live in Africa for a full year, *concerned* about the security challenges that were presented by the civil war, and *anxious* to see what opportunities awaited me on these roads less traveled.

Juba's layout was dramatic: unpaved roads, modern hotels, and lots of unfinished construction set against a backdrop of beautiful mountains on its outskirts, dotted with vegetation. Within the city borders, traditional earthen *tukuls* punctuated the landscape even near the airport. The Nile channels life through Juba and provides picturesque views for the restaurants scattered along it.

South Sudan's culinary history traces back thousands of years with ties from Ancient Egypt, East Africa, and the Arabian Peninsula. The nation's food reflects the heart and soul of its people: resilient, bold, and proudly, unapologetically, and beautifully African. I learned just how strong one's tribal identity influenced all aspects of life. After engaging with members of the nation's various tribes (including members of my office team) it became clear that there are two distinct types of cooking in South Sudan. Nomadic tribes primarily rear cattle as their source of income and also utilize it as the base for their food. Beef and dairy are the primary sources of diet. Those tribes that live in the lush green areas of the country are agrarian and tend to utilize local greens and root vegetables, along with meat and fish as key components to their cuisine. I was told that the non-herding tribes of the country tend to eat more vegetables while the nomadic herding tribes rely primarily on cattle because growing vegetables would require staying in one spot for an entire growing season, from seed to harvest - something that nomads don't do.

It took me about three months to host a cooking tutorial dinner party with locals and some of my embassy friends; it's something I often do when in a foreign country. As long as you take time to get to know your new friends, there's no harm in opening up your home for culinary explorations! I wanted to learn how to cook native South Sudanese dishes, so what did I do? I befriended locals and invited them to my home to cook! Let your home be the meeting-plane that transports you to distant lands.

A mixture of afro beats and reggae filled the air of my small shipping container-turned-apartment, as my three friends began creating an unforgettable dinner. Within an hour they created three traditional dishes served with local bread. The dish that captured my heart was salata aswad (translated "eggplant salad"). It was completely new and unexpected. I knew the taste of eggplant, but mixing it with the creaminess of peanut butter provided another dimension. It might be foreign to the typical Western palate, but the peanut butter provides the right element to hold all the other ingredients together with the eggplant. Trust me. Once I tasted it I knew I would incorporate it into my cooking catalogue. One of the most memorable things about that day cooking with my South Sudanese friends was their parting gift. They left their traditional stirring spoons with me as keepsakes. These long wooden sticks with a hammerhead shape at the end are now a permanent part of my kitchen, used to create many dishes!

SALATA ASWAD

PREP
45 mins.

COOK
0

SKILL LEVEL
Easy

SERVES
8-10

AFRICA

INGREDIENTS

- 4 medium sized eggplants
- ¼ cup olive oil
- 2 large tomatoes
- 1 large red onion
- 1 large, peeled cucumber
- 2 cloves garlic
- ½ tsp. black pepper
- ½ tsp. cumin seeds
- 1 tsp. salt
- 1 cup feta cheese
- 1 cup plain yogurt
- 2 tbsp. unsweetened natural peanut butter
- ½ lemon (juice)

INSTRUCTIONS

Peel and dice the eggplant in large portions and soak them for 10 minutes in salt water. Pat dry with a towel.

Heat olive oil in a frying pan and fry eggplant until golden brown (20-25 minutes). *Do not place all eggplant in oil at the same time, fry in three separate batches to ensure their crispiness.*

Place eggplant aside to cool.

Dice tomatoes, onions, and cucumber, then place in a bowl together. In a separate bowl mix peanut butter, salt, and yogurt along with chopped garlic.

Mix eggplant with ingredients mentioned above in a large bowl and add black pepper, lemon juice and feta cheese. Garnish with cilantro.

Chef's tip: Please use the most natural, unprocessed peanut butter you can find. Commercially processed peanut butter has added sugars and fillers that will alter the dish's flavors. The more natural your peanut butter is, the better the dish will taste.

JEREMIAH KNIGHT

SOUTH SUDANESE PEANUT CREAMED SPINACH

PREP	COOK	SKILL LEVEL	SERVES
25 mins.	10-12 mins.	Easy	4-6

INGREDIENTS

- 3 large bunches of whole leaf (large stem) spinach
- ¾ cup water
- 1 large red onion, diced
- ¾ teaspoon fine sea salt
- pinch of black pepper to taste (or grains of paradise)
- ½ cup of natural smooth peanut butter (no sugar added)
- 1 large tomato, diced
- 2 cloves of garlic (crushed)
- 2 tbsp. of olive oil

INSTRUCTIONS

Rinse and dry spinach and chop thinly.

Saute on medium heat onions and garlic in a pot until they become translucent. (approximately 5 minutes)

Add water to the pot and heat until boiling.

Add the chopped spinach, salt, and black pepper.

Cook, stirring down the spinach until it is all wilted and still bright green - 3 to 4 minutes.

Add in peanut butter and stir.

Add in diced tomatoes and stir. If the mixture is too thick, add some additional water.

Serve stew warm as a side or main dish.

EGYPT

I remember deciding at the last minute to visit Egypt. This trip was a needed escape from long hours and extended work weeks that accompanied my time in Juba. It was my first getaway after being in the country for 5 months. The fresh sea air of Sharm el Sheikh, the golden reflections of desert sands, and a bounty of fish and seafood were just what the doctor ordered to energize me.

I threw some things into a bag without paying much attention. I figured that Egypt was just two countries north of South Sudan, so the temperature couldn't possibly change that much – I was wrong! I remember being so cold in Egypt that I rushed into a local shop to buy a light jacket on my first night out.

Sneak tip: Being multilingual, I pretended I was from a Spanish-speaking country to avoid paying a higher price as an American, (It worked! I got a great deal - or at least I think I did).

Sharm el Sheikh, located on the Red Sea portion of the Sinai Peninsula, is a seafood lover's oasis. I quickly began asking hotel staff, taxi drivers, shop owners, and local residents about where I could find the best seafood in the city (locals are always the best guides). The general consensus was that Fares Seafood Restaurant was the place to go. Upon entering I knew I was in the right place because the establishment had very few foreigners! It was full of Egyptians - a telltale sign of authenticity. I chose a fresh sea bass prepared in the *samak mashwi* style. Translated *grilled fish*; this is one of the classic ways Egyptians enjoy cooking their seafood. With its rooftop view; melodic sounds pouring out of storefronts below; and the air perfumed with charred herbs, cardamom, cinnamon, and savory scents of fish and lamb, the restaurant was the perfect setting in which to enjoy a perfect meal.

During the remainder of my time in Egypt I explored all the delicacies the Red Sea and Sinai Peninsula had to offer. Through them I could see, taste, and feel the evolution of humanity. Because of Egypt's history of conquering, being conquered, and becoming a metropolis for immigrants during the Roman Empire, its cuisine is a clear reflection of the march of time. You can experience classic Egyptian dishes that have been enjoyed for thousands of years, alongside those from the newer Roman, Ottoman and British empires. If you can't make it to Egypt to experience it for yourself, you might want to make my interpretation of *samak mashwi* – it's guaranteed to be a crowd pleaser!

SAMAK MASHWI

PREP
30 mins.

COOK
30-40 mins.

SKILL LEVEL
Easy

SERVES
2

AFRICA

INGREDIENTS

- 2 medium (about 2.5 lb.) whole striped bass, sea bass or red snapper (gutted and cleaned)
- sea salt
- ½ lemon

Rub/Marinade:
- 1 lemon and 2 limes (juice)
- 5 cloves garlic
- 2 tbsp. olive oil
- ¼ cup chopped chives
- ¼ cup chopped cilantro
- 1 tbsp. ground cumin
- 2-3 tbsp. fresh oregano
- 1 red chili pepper, finely chopped
- sea salt
- white peppercorns (crushed and to taste)

Other Ingredients:
- 1 cup all purpose flour
- a couple of fresh thyme twigs
- a couple of fresh rosemary twigs

Wine and Garlic Sauce:
- 1 medium head garlic
- 2 tbsp. unsalted butter
- ¼ cup chicken stock
- ¼ cup dry white wine
- 3 limes (juice)
- salt and black pepper to taste

INSTRUCTIONS

Clean the fish by rubbing it with salt and half a lemon. Rinse with water, and pat dry with a clean towel.

For the marinade: Combine all the ingredients and pour into a food processor, pulsing just a few times to get it to an even consistency. Set this mixture aside.

Mix ingredients for wine sauce in a small saucepan and place over a medium heat for 10 minutes. Let it rest during the fish cooking process.

With a spoon, fill the fish with ¾ of the marinade mixture. Close the fish and cut three diagonal slits into the skin, penetrating the flesh. Fill the slits with the remaining rub/marinade. Do this to both sides of the fish. For the best flavor, cover the fish and place in the refrigerator to marinate overnight. Otherwise, let the fish marinate for 30 minutes.

Take the fish out of the fridge and gently roll in flour. This prevents the fish from burning and drying out on the grill. Place sprigs of fresh thyme and rosemary directly on top of the fish.

Place the fish inside a grilling basket (if not directly on the grill) and cook each side on medium high heat for 15 to 20 minutes, depending on the size of the fish.

Once the fish is almost cooked, reheat the sauce.

As soon as you remove the fish from the grill, pour the hot wine and garlic sauce over the fish.

Chef's tip: The key to making this dish turn out right is to make sure that you pack all the seasoning in the fish. Don't rush the process. The longer you let the seasoning marinate in the fish, the better it will taste. Also, like I say with all fish and seafood, NEVER OVERCOOK IT! Even though the recipe says 15-20 minutes, depending on the heat of the grill, I would rather take it off early and let it rest to finish cooking than risk having it dry out.

EGYPTIAN FALAFEL

PREP	COOK	SKILL LEVEL	SERVES
40 mins.	10 mins.	Easy	15-18 pieces

INGREDIENTS

- 1 cup dried fava beans, soaked overnight (or chick-peas for the traditional style)
- ½ cup red onion (chopped)
- ½ bunch(½ cup) flat leaf parsley, chopped
- ½ bunch (½ cup) cilantro, chopped
- 1 small chile pepper
- 3 garlic cloves
- 1 tsp. cumin
- 1½ tsp. ground coriander
- 1½ tsp. salt
- ½ tsp. black cardamom (if you don't have black just use green)
- 2 tbsp. chickpea flour
- ½ tsp. baking soda
- vegetable oil for frying

INSTRUCTIONS

Place fava beans in a large bowl and cover with several inches of water. Let soak, 8 hours to overnight. Drain.

Combine soaked fava beans, red onion, parsley, cilantro, garlic, coriander, salt, and cumin in a food processor; process to a dough-like consistency.

Use your hands, an ice cream scoop or falafel scoop to form the falafel into balls. If you find the mixture is too wet, you can add another tablespoon of chickpea flour. If it's too dry and crumbly, you can add a teaspoon or two of water.

Fill a deep frying pan ¼ full with oil; heat over medium heat. Fry balls in batches until golden brown, 3 to 5 minutes. Drain on paper towels. Serve warm with pita bread.

YANSOON

Though this drink is traditionally served hot, I think it is perfect to serve chilled on a warm summer day. You can always edit the recipe and serve it hot if desired.

PREP	COOK	SKILL LEVEL	SERVES
10 mins.	0	Easy	3

INGREDIENTS

- 2 cups water
- 2 tsp. aniseed
- 2 tsp. honey (or more to taste)
- 1 tsp. lime juice (my spin on it!)
- 4 ice cubes

INSTRUCTIONS

Boil ingredients except lime juice for 2 minutes.

Pour through strainer and add lime juice.

Add ice cubes and serve chilled.

Information

ALGERIA

I have known my close friend Lawrence since my first year of undergraduate studies at Morehouse College. Like me, he has spent his life traveling the world and exploring what humanity has to offer. I credit him with introducing me to international affairs and diplomacy. When I told him about this cookbook, he kindly offered to share his experience with Algerian cuisine. As an international diplomacy officer, he has spent many years in the Arab-speaking world and has lived in Algeria on two occasions. It was during his first stay in Algeria that he was introduced to *shakshouka* (locally known as *tchektchouka*), a savory dish of eggs poached in a spiced tomato sauce. Lawrence told me it's eaten all of the time, and generally served as an easy meal when having people over.

Shakshouka also makes for a wonderful family-style meal, and the best thing about family-style eating is, well, family! To me there is no better way to enjoy a meal than with family and friends digging into the same dishes and having an amazing conversation to spice things up. With good conversation, every meal has some element of "family" in it.

When it comes to *shakshouka*, I personally find this simple and fresh dish useful, not only as a starter but also as a quick main dish when accompanied with fresh French bread and a simple arugula salad!

LAWRENCE'S SHAKSHOUKA

PREP
10 mins.

COOK
25-30 mins.

SKILL LEVEL
Easy

SERVES
6

INGREDIENTS

- 1 tbsp. olive oil
- 1 large yellow onion, peeled and diced
- 2 cloves garlic, minced
- 1 medium green pepper diced
- 1 medium red pepper
- 1 medium yellow pepper
- 4 cups ripe diced tomatoes, or 2 cans (14 oz. each) diced tomatoes
- 2 tbsp. tomato paste
- 1 tsp. cumin
- 1 tsp. paprika
- a pinch nutmeg
- salt and pepper to taste
- 4-5 eggs
- 3 tbsp. of fresh chopped parsley (1 tbsp. reserved for garnish)
- ½ tbsp. of fresh mint

AFRICA

INSTRUCTIONS

Sauté onions and garlic in olive oil in a saucepan until translucent.

Add the diced peppers with parsley to the saucepan and cook for about 5-6 minutes.

Add diced tomatoes and cook for an additional 5-6 minutes.

Add tomato paste and cook for an additional 5 minutes.

Crack the eggs, one at a time, directly over the tomato mixture, making sure to space them evenly over the sauce.

Cover pan, lower heat and cook for about 10 minutes.

Garnish with chopped parsley and mint.

Chef's tip: a simple arugula salad should consist of fresh arugula, dressed with a mix of lime juice, olive oil, sea salt, freshly grated Romano cheese, and coarsely ground black pepper to taste. Simple and to the point!

CHERBET BOUFARIK

PREP	COOK	SKILL LEVEL	SERVES
20 mins.	0	Easy	10

INGREDIENTS

- 1 cup fresh lemon juice
- zest of one lemon
- 2 cups granulated sugar
- ¼ cup whole milk (dairy free: substitute coconut milk)
- 2 tbsp. orange blossom water
- mint for garnish (optional)
- 10-12 cups water

INSTRUCTIONS

Add lemon zest to 5 cups of water and sugar. Bring to a boil and then reduce to a low simmer for approximately 5 mins. Allow the mixture to cool.

Strain cooled mixture and add in orange blossom water and the remaining water along with milk.

Place in the refrigerator until chill and ready to drink.

Serve in glass with ice and garnish with mint if desired.

SOUTH AFRICA

As the "Southern Gateway to Africa", South Africa's people, landscape, and food, represent some of the best of the continent. From its urban hipster centers found in Johannesburg, to the picturesque vineyards of Cape Town, at times I found myself overwhelmed by the abundance of flavors the land had to offer.

One day at a traditional Cape Town restaurant, I opted for their version of apple pie and ice cream. I absolutely love hot apple pie and ice cream. I love it so much I make it a point to always try it on any menu I come across. However, my dear South African friend Karabo ordered malva pudding, South Africa's answer to British sticky toffee pudding. What happened next seemed insignificant but was so important: *my friend and I tried each-others' desserts.* One thing about me is that I'm a firm believer that food is meant to be shared! I hate when my dining friends don't want to try out what I ordered or refuse to share what they've ordered. I believe that the whole eating process is communal. I truly believe in "breaking bread" together; what's mine (and yours) is *ours.* So many discoveries happen when sharing food at the dinner table.

The apple pie I ordered was okay, but with one spoonful of malva pudding, I instantly fell in love. I thought it would be just a bland pound cake with a sauce. Boy, was I wrong! It was a flavorful dessert that harmoniously merged a caramel-like base (one of my favorite flavors) with fruit (apricot preserve). That is a match made in heaven. I ended up eating more of Karabo's dessert than my own-which, come to think of it, might be why some folks don't like sharing. I still encourage it though!

Following our dinner, we visited an old friend of mine named Kim. At that moment, she worked in the U.S. Consulate in Cape Town. I raved to her about my instant love for malva pudding and, to my surprise, she had a mutual infatuation – she even gifted me with her favorite malva pudding recipe! Of course, being the culinary fusionist I am, I adjusted it in the recipe for the Caribbean soul that resides within me: I substituted apricot jam for guava and mango jam. I also included brown sugar (widely used as a sweetener in the Caribbean) as well as nutmeg in the sauce to give it an additional Caribbean flair. Karabo suddenly passed in December of 2021, this recipe is in honor of you! Please have some waiting for me when I see you in heaven. I hope you, my readers, enjoy this as much as I do!"

JEREMIAH'S MALVA PUDDING

PREP
15-20 mins.

COOK
30-45 mins.

SKILL LEVEL
Medium

SERVES
8

INGREDIENTS

- ½ cup white sugar
- ¼ cup brown sugar (my addition)
- 2 large eggs
- 3 tsp. apricot jam
- 2 tsp. mango jam
- 1 tsp. white wine vinegar
- 2 tbsp. melted unsalted butter
- 1⅓ cup flour
- a pinch of salt
- 1 tsp. baking soda
- ½ cup milk

Sauce:

- 1¾ cup whole milk (or a little more depending on how moist you want it)
- a dash of vanilla almond extract (my addition)
- 4½ oz. butter
- ¼ cup white sugar
- ½ tsp. nutmeg (my addition)

AFRICA

INSTRUCTIONS

Preheat oven to 300⁰ F. Grease a rectangular pie dish.

Using a handheld mixer, whip eggs and sugar until light and fluffy.

Mix butter, jam, and vinegar together. Then add to the egg mixture, stirring well during the process.

Sift the dry ingredients together. Alternately, fold the dry ingredients and milk into the egg mixture.

Pour batter into the pie dish and bake for 30-45 minutes until golden brown. Cool completely.

For the sauce: add all ingredients to a saucepan. Melt them at low heat. Whisk until the sugar dissolves, allow to simmer for 5 minutes before removing from heat.

Immediately as the pudding is pulled from the oven, pour the warm sauce over it and allow it to sit for at least 10 minutes.

Serve warm with a spoonful of homemade whipped cream, vanilla cream sauce, or vanilla ice cream.

CHAKALAKA

PREP	COOK	SKILL LEVEL	SERVES
20 mins.	15 mins.	Easy	2-4

INGREDIENTS

- 2 cups grated carrots
- 1(15oz.) can of beans
- ½ red pepper, finely chopped
- ½ green pepper, finely chopped
- 1 yellow pepper, finely chopped
- 2 chili peppers, finely chopped
- 1 medium white onion, diced
- 3 tbsp. curry powder
- 1 tbsp. sea salt
- 1 tbsp. black pepper
- 3 tbsp. olive oil
- 3 cloves of garlic, finely chopped
- 2 tsp. ginger root, chopped
- 1 tsp. paprika

INSTRUCTIONS

Fry chilies, peppers & onions in the oil.

Add ginger, paprika & garlic.

Add curry powder.

Add carrots and cook for 10 minutes.

Add salt and pepper to taste, then add baked beans and cook for 5 minutes.

Serve hot or cold.

ASIA & OCEANI

FIJI | INDONESIA | PAKISTAN | THAILAND | TURKEY

A

FIJI

As the coastline of Fiji welcomed me from my aerial view it was every bit of a dream come true. I'd been acquainted with Fiji since childhood as my father's National Geographic subscription served as my window into Micronesian, Melanesian, and Polynesian areas of the Pacific. I'd been spellbound for decades.

Hands down, Fijians are some of the nicest people in the entire world. Every time you pass someone on the streets you are greeted warmly, strangers are more than happy to help you find your way if you're lost, and their professional customer service is second to none. In fact, once at dinner I asked our waiter a simple question about sightseeing and ended up getting invited to a full, private tour of the city plus a legendary kava ceremony! We've kept in touch since. Fiji feels like home in more ways than one.

I quickly found that Fiji has many strong culinary linkages to the Caribbean culture I grew up with. Mangoes and, other tropical fruits, ground provisions like cassava, and the large variety of, fresh fish and seafood all felt so familiar. During my stay, I recognized that there were two distinct types of Fijian cuisine. There's the traditional Fijian cuisine created by the original inhabitants of the island (often using banana leaves and hot stones in the cooking process) and there is the Indo-Fijian cuisine created by the migrants from India who arrived in the late 1800s. I found that Indo-Fijian cuisine is much spicier and of course, is based on its Indian heritage while incorporating local produce. As for the traditional Fijian cuisine, a common thread is its extensive use of the coconut. Most of Fiji's popular dishes have found a way to incorporate some part of the coconut, and for that I am forever grateful. Fijians love their coconut, and so do I!

Kokoda, the South Pacific's response to ceviche, uses coconut milk for a rich and unexpected flavor, leaving you wanting more and more. But by far my favorite Fijian dish is rourou (the Fijian word for taro leaves). I think I ordered it every day while I was visiting!

KOKODA

PREP
15-20 mins.

COOK
0

SKILL LEVEL
Easy

SERVES
6-8

ASIA & OCEANIA

INGREDIENTS

- 1 tbsp. olive oil
- 1 lb. fresh snapper fillet (or any fresh fish), skinned and cut into ½ inch pieces
- 3 limes (juice)
- 5 lemons (juice)
- 1 medium-sized red onion (finely diced)
- 1 red chili pepper (finely sliced, optional)
- 1 green chili pepper (finely sliced, optional... I like to add it for an extra bit of heat)
- 1 large tomato (seeds removed, finely chopped)
- 3 scallions (thinly sliced)
- ¼ cup cilantro finely chopped
- 1 small yellow bell pepper (chopped with seeds removed)
- 2 cups of coconut milk
- sea salt to taste
- lime wedges to serve

INSTRUCTIONS

In a bowl, mix the fish and the lemon/lime juice to marinate for 30 mins. Reserve about ¼ cup of lemon/lime juice.

Rinse and drain the fish in cold water.

Add remaining ingredients along with the reserved lemon/lime juice.

Chef's tip: You have to eat kokoda the same day you make it. Do not put it in the refrigerator. The oils from the coconut milk will solidify and become clumpy - something you definitely do not want to partake of the next day. If possible, you can buy a fresh coconut, grate it, and strain the coconut milk from the pulp. This is the more traditional preparation; trust me it tastes even better.

ROUROU

 PREP	 COOK	 SKILL LEVEL	 SERVES
15-20 mins.	10 mins.	Easy	4

INGREDIENTS

- 20 young taro rourou leaves, chopped finely (you can substitute spinach)
- 1 medium onion
- 1 tomato
- 4 cloves garlic, crushed
- 2 tbsp. coconut oil
- 3 tsp. baking soda
- salt to taste

INSTRUCTIONS

Boil rourou, add baking soda and cook until soft.

Ensure there is just enough water added to cook the rourou, as you don't want any water left after the rourou is cooked. If there is leftover water in the rourou, use the strainer to drain the water out.

In a frying pan, add oil, onion, tomato and garlic, and fry until golden brown.

Add cooked rourou and stir through.

Add salt to taste and serve warm.

INDONESIA

I had just finished passing through customs with my bags and was looking for my driver to take me to the hotel in Jakarta. Flashing sirens caught the corner of my eye as I glanced at a nearby TV; to my astonishment, military tanks were surrounding the presidential palace. Abdurrahman Wahid had been removed as president yet refused to leave. When my driver finally pulled up, I was quickly whisked away to my hotel, but in the morning my trip was adjusted to address the uncertainties of the political environment. Fears of security breaches meant I wasn't able to explore the city as much as I would have liked to, but we were still allowed a little bit of time to enjoy our stay.

I was in Jakarta as part of my apprenticeship with the London headquarters of the British Multinational Oil and Gas company BP. My boss suggested I attend a global leadership workshop in Indonesia and of course I jumped at that offer. We had a carefully curated introduction to Indonesia's people, culture and food. I returned to the hotel with the taste and cultural immersion of the night settled in my belly, and I vividly remember the kindness of the hotel's staff. They were excited to share their local fruits and encouraged me to try a variety of local dishes. I told them how much I enjoyed trying chicken satay, and also Asian pears for the first time that night. The next morning a large bowl of the most beautiful Asian pears was waiting for me at the door of my hotel room. What fantastic hospitality!

That morning, in addition to the wonderful gift of fresh fruit, I awoke to great news: President Wahid relinquished his claim to power and for the first time in Indonesia's history, a woman was sworn in as president! When I think of Indonesia, my mind always goes back to when I witnessed the nation's fight to protect its democracy.

INDONESIAN SATAY AYAM

PREP
1 hour 30 mins.

COOK
30-45 mins.

SKILL LEVEL
Medium

SERVES
15-20

ASIA & OCEANIA

INGREDIENTS

- 50 wooden bamboo skewers
- 2 lb. chicken, cubed

Marinade:
- ½ cup sweet soy sauce
- 3 garlic cloves, finely minced
- 2 or 3 shallots, sliced thin
- 2 tbsp. regular soy sauce
- 2 red chilies, diced
- 1 tsp. smoked paprika
- ¼ tsp. white pepper, ground
- 2 tsp. turmeric
- 2 tsp. ground coriander
- 2 tsp. ground nutmeg
- 1 tsp. ground cumin
- 1 tsp. garlic powder
- 1 tbs. olive oil
- 1 tsp. salt
- 2 tsp. liquid smoke (optional)

Basting Sauce:
- ¼ cup Kecap Manis (Indonesian sweet soy sauce) or just add 3 tbsp. brown sugar to regular soy sauce
- 1 lime (juice)
- ¼ cup cilantro
- 1 tsp. shrimp paste
- 1 shallot, sliced thin

INSTRUCTIONS

Cube the chicken into slightly smaller than 1 in. cubes (about 2 cm). Soak the bamboo skewers for ½ hour in water prior to impaling the chicken cubes and putting on the grill. This way they won't burn.

Prepare both the basting mix and the marinade by mixing their ingredients in two different bowls.

Place the cubed chicken into marinade bowl and let marinate, preferably overnight but at least for several hours. Take the marinated meat cubes and stick them on the skewers, about 4 or 5 per stick. If you are unable to grill outside, add about 2 teaspoons of liquid smoke.

Prepare the grill, (charcoal is preferable, but a large griddle/pan can also substitute). When heat is even, place skewered meat on the grilling surface.

Baste the meat initially and continue to turn every 2 minutes until fully cooked while basting at the top of each flip.

Serve alone or with a peanut sauce.

Chef's tip: I particularly like to mix both dark and white meat when making satay. You don't want your satay coming out dry, which happens easily with white meat. Adding the dark meat (which has some fat in it) keeps it nice and juicy. You want to make sure it is not pink on the inside but you also don't want to overcook it. It should be tender and juicy, not dry and hard. If you have a high flame, you will need to turn the meat more frequently to prevent overcooking.

BAJIGUR

PREP	COOK	SKILL LEVEL	SERVES
5 mins.	15 mins.	Easy	4-5

INGREDIENTS

- 2 tbsp. black coffee
- 1 cup water
- 4 cups coconut milk
- ½ cup brown sugar
- 2 tbsp. fresh chopped ginger
- 1 vanilla bean (traditionally 2 sheets of pandan leaves would be used)
- 1 stalk of lemongrass
- a dash of salt

INSTRUCTIONS

Boil together ginger, cinnamon, lemongrass, and pandan leaves (if you use the vanilla bean, please split the vanilla bean open before boiling).

Add brown sugar and black coffee and stir well.

Lower heat, add coconut milk and bring to a nice simmer for about 10 minutes.

Strain and serve hot.

PAKISTAN

It was a sweltering summer evening that must have been at least 110 degrees Fahrenheit when I made my first trip from Pakistan's capital, Islamabad to its neighboring city Rawalipindi for an unforgettable night. Upon arriving at my friend's home, it became very clear that this was going to be a culinary adventure to remember. After having a seat in the formal living room for conversation, the savory scents escaping the kitchen of this 200-year-old home began to find their way into my nostrils and, eventually, my stomach and heart. Soon after, I was invited to the backyard patio where dinner would be served under the moon on a starlit summer's evening.

The table spread was second to none, with candles perfectly placed between the assorted dishes. By flickering flames, we laughed and ate for what seemed like an eternity. We shared our stories of mutual passion for food and the cultures that shaped them. I have never experienced such clear distinctions in regional cuisines like those in Pakistan. Its four provinces and federal territory boast their own unique culinary traditions. During my time living in Pakistan, I made it a point to explore them as best as I could. Living in a country whose borders house one of the cradles of civilization, I was also exposed to ancient cooking techniques that have endured the test of time. Cooking Pakistani food is not for a novice, but by the same token, it's welcoming to all those who are brave enough to explore. Don't let complexity in a nation's culinary style deter you from experiencing something new. Rather, see it as a challenge to improve on your skills!

No matter where I am in the world, when I cook chicken biryani, the kitchen magically converts to that centuries-old home in Pakistan that provided the perfect introduction to Pakistani cuisine for me. To me, biryani speaks to all that is Pakistan. It's a dish that incorporates the distinct flavor of basmati rice and envelopes it with richly spiced meat and yogurt – a perfect show of how Pakistani cuisine stands in a league of its own. Many cultures have rice and meat dishes. However, none can come even close to the Sindh region's spicy version of biryani. So I share with you my take on this quintessential Pakistani dish…Sindh chicken biryani!

SINDH CHICKEN BIRYANI

PREP
5-6 hours

COOK
30-40 mins.

SKILL LEVEL
Difficult

SERVES
8-10

INGREDIENTS

- 2 lb. chicken, cut into about 8 large chunks

Marinade:
- ¼ cup yogurt
- 1 tsp. ginger paste
- 1 tsp. garlic paste
- 2 tbsp. coconut oil
- 1 tsp. red chili powder
- ½ tsp. turmeric powder
- 1 green chili, chopped
- 1 tsp. salt

Other Ingredients:
- 5 cups long grain basmati rice
- ½ cup cooking oil
- 6 medium red onions, sliced
- 4 medium tomatoes, finely diced
- 10 dried prunes, soaked in warm water for 5 minutes
- 2-4 green chilies, chopped
- 1 cup fresh plain yogurt
- 2 tsp. fresh garlic, crushed into a paste
- 2 tsp. fresh ginger, crushed into a paste
- 1 tsp. salt, or to taste
- 1 tsp. red chili powder
- ½ tsp. turmeric powder
- 1 tsp. garam masala
- 8 cloves
- 2 green cardamom pods
- 2 black cardamom pods
- 5 black peppercorns
- 2 tsp. cumin seeds
- 2 cinnamon sticks
- 2 bay leaves
- 2 tbsp. fresh mint, chopped
- 2 tbsp. fresh cilantro, chopped
- 1 tsp. saffron, crushed and soaked in warm water
- 1 small lime
- ¼ cup of cashews

INSTRUCTIONS

Allow the chicken to marinate overnight in the refrigerator with the marinade. Make sure to rub the chicken well with the marinade. Don't be shy, get your fingers dirty!

Wash and then soak the rice for about 20-30 minutes.

Fry onions in oil until they turn golden and crispy. Remove a quarter of the fried onions (these will be used later) and leave the rest in the pan. Add the whole spices (cumin, cardamom, 4 cloves, bay leaves, cinnamon and black pepper). Sauté the spices and the onions until their fragrance becomes strong and they begin to sizzle.

Add garlic and ginger pastes (both are simply made by pounding them into a paste or placing them in a food processor).

Next, add tomatoes, prunes, turmeric, salt and red chili powder.

Cook mixture for 10-15 minutes. Add in green chilis and chicken. Allow the meat to cook in the tomato mixture for a few minutes, then add the additional whipped yogurt plus the saffron mixture, and mix well. Then add about a half cup of water and cook until the meat is tender and the sauce becomes nice and thick.

Bring a large pot of water to boil, add about 2 tbsp. salt, 2 tbsp. oil and additional two pieces of cardamom, one cinnamon stick and 3-4 cloves. Add in the already drained, soaked rice and cook until ¾ of the way done (about 6-8 minutes). Drain off water.

Layer the meat with rice, sprinkle the reserved fried onions on each layer along with chopped cilantro and mint. Cover with a tight lid and place on very low heat for about 15 minutes to steam. Once done, open and fluff up the biryani gently. Add the juice of one small lime.

Chef's tip: In the final cooking portion of the recipe, cover the pot with at least two layers of foil, cling them tightly around and then place the lid on. It helps with the steaming process and makes the rice nice and fluffy. I like extremely low heat for this, so it may take a bit more than 15 minutes. Biryani should not be rushed. The longer it takes, the better it tastes. Also please use fresh herbs! It makes the flavor so much better.

MANGO LASSI

PREP
15 mins.

COOK
0

SKILL LEVEL
Easy

SERVES
1-2

INGREDIENTS

- 1 cup plain yogurt
- ½ cup fresh ripe mango (can be substituted with frozen pulp)
- ½ cup milk
- 3 tbsp. sugar
- ¼ tsp. rosewater essence

INSTRUCTIONS

Add all the ingredients into a blender and blend until all combined.

Add crushed ice into a glass and pour Lassi.

Note: If you like your Lassi a bit thinner in consistency, you can add more milk and mango pulp. You can adjust the sweetness as well by adding or reducing sugar.

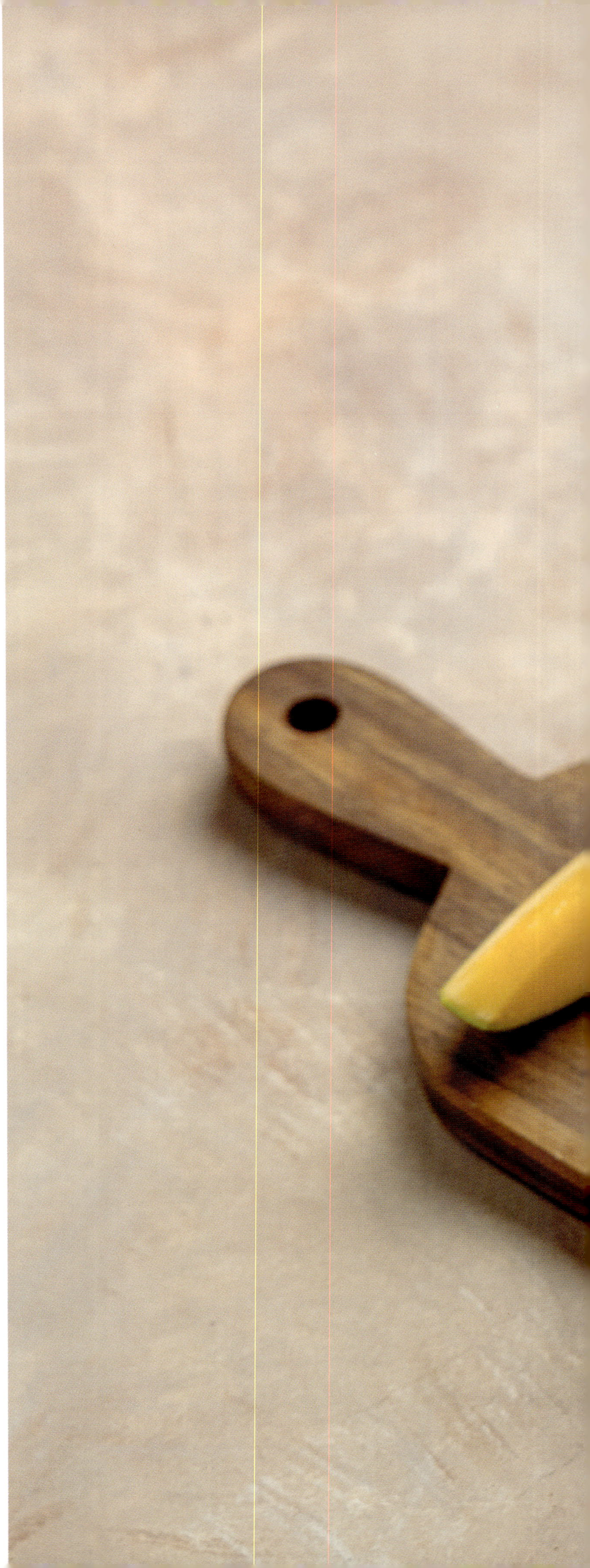

GARLIC AND CHIVE CHAPATI

PREP
15-20 mins.

COOK
3 mins.

SKILL LEVEL
Easy

SERVES
2

INGREDIENTS

- 2 cups wheat flour
- 2 tsp. vegetable oil
- salt to taste
- water as needed
- 2 cloves garlic, crushed
- 2 tsp. fresh chives, chopped
- 2 tsp. butter

INSTRUCTIONS

Melt butter in a frying pan. Then add in chopped garlic and sauté for about 3-4 minutes.

Transfer garlic to a separate bowl.

In the same bowl add wheat flour and chives.

Gradually add in water while mixing. Continue to mix until dough becomes a ball that is not sticky and can be kneaded.

Cover dough and place to rest for 15-20 minutes.

Create small balls and roll them out until they are thin.

At medium temperature, heat oil in a large frying pan.

Cook on both sides until golden brown.

Finish off with a spread of butter on the top side.

THAILAND

I had the opportunity to visit Thailand for a five-day vacation. It was just enough time to make a few new friends and learn about hidden eateries tucked far away from the beaten paths of tourist traps. I asked my tour guide if she knew of a nice beach near the capital. She told me that there were none close by but by the end of our conversation she arranged for her boyfriend to drive me to the beach the following day. It was about an hour or so away from Bangkok — what a testament to the hospitality of Thai people! Some might fear hopping into cars with strangers, but I tend to go by people's vibe. A general attitude of distrust will keep you from having some of the best times of your life!

The next day her boyfriend took me to Pattaya City where we enjoyed a boat ride to one of the most beautiful little islands I have ever seen. I then headed back to hang out with their friends, eating, laughing, and making lifelong memories. We have kept in touch for years since that experience. Thai people are amazing, and their recommendations rarely miss!

But the following day when my driver pulled up to a restaurant recommended to me by my new local friends, I was a bit skeptical. My favorite foreign spots are usually sidewalk food carts and obscure two-table mom and pop shops. This Thai restaurant looked rather upscale and swanky. However, I'm glad I didn't let my silly assumptions keep me from enjoying one of my favorite meals ever! It's true that foreign cuisine can be high-end and upscale while still being authentic. That night's dinner has been forever etched in my mind. In particular, the Tahi Pad Kra Pao Ga, a flavorful spiced basil chicken, was the crowning jewel of my evening. With only three days left in my trip, I spent the remainder of my time in Thailand ordering the dish at every opportunity in search of my favorite (version of it).

RESTAURANT

THAI PAD KRA PAO GA

PREP
20 mins.

COOK
15 mins.

SKILL LEVEL
Medium

SERVES
2

INGREDIENTS

- 1 chicken breast, or any other cut of boneless chicken (can also substitute 11 oz. of ground pork or about 12 fresh peeled-and-cleaned shrimp)
- 4 cloves garlic
- 3-6 Thai red chilies
- 3 green chilies
- 3 tbsp. coconut oil for frying
- 1 tsp. of oyster sauce
- 1 tsp. light soy sauce
- 1 splash mushroom flavored dark soy sauce
- 1 tsp. sugar
- 1 handful Thai holy basil leaves (can substitute for Thai basil)
- 1 egg
- 1 clove garlic

INSTRUCTIONS

With a mortar and pestle, pound the red chilies and 4 cloves of garlic together until the mix forms a rough looking paste. Set the paste aside.

Remove leaves of basil from the stalk and place in a bowl.

Dice meat into very small pieces (for shrimp you can leave them whole).

Add oil to a large frying pan or wok and place over high heat (but don't add meat yet).

When the oil is hot, add the chilies and garlic. Stir fry them for about 20 seconds until they get really fragrant, but don't let them burn or get too dry.

Add in meat and cook for about 2 minutes with the stock.

Add remaining ingredients (excluding the basil, egg, and extra clove of garlic) and cook for about one minute on high flame.

Turn off flame (if using an electric stove, remove from heat) and add in the basil. Fold the basil into the chicken and let sit for about 2-3 minutes.

Fried Egg
Heat about 2 tablespoons of coconut oil in a wok or frying pan on medium-high heat.

Slice the extra clove of garlic into three parts and place in oil.

When garlic becomes a golden brown, drop in the egg.

Do not turn the egg over but cook until white part becomes solid.

Remove from oil and place on paper towels.

Add on top of chicken.

Serve with Jasmine rice (optional).

Chef's tip: When using the mortar and pestle to mix the chilies and garlic, I like to add a pinch or two of sea salt to it. It helps release more of the natural oils into the mixture.

SWEET COCONUT STICKY RICE

I can truly say that I ate my way through Thailand. I could not sum up my experience with its culinary offerings by sharing just one dish. One of my favorite desserts in Thailand is a rice dessert made with coconut milk. I love, LOVE coconut milk, so this dessert did not have to fight for my affection! It is a great dish to infuse into your Caribbean or Subcontinental meals. So of course, I am going to share my version, which has a little twist to it (addition of elderflower cordial).

PREP	COOK	SKILL LEVEL	SERVES
5 mins.	20 mins.	Medium	4

INGREDIENTS

- 2 tbsp. coriander seeds
- 1 cup glutinous or sticky rice
- ½ can unsweetened coconut milk
- ⅔ cup water
- ½ tsp. sea salt
- ½ tsp. ginger, freshly grated
- 1 tsp. elderflower cordial (my addition)

INSTRUCTIONS

Rinse rice with several changes of water until water is no longer cloudy.

Place coconut milk, water, ginger, coriander seeds, elderflower cordial and salt to a small pot. Add rice and bring to a boil.

Cover, reduce heat to lowest setting and allow to steam for 20 minutes. Remove cover, fluff rice with a fork.

Serve while warm with slices of mango (optional).

EURO

AUSTRIA | BELGIUM | FRANCE | INCELAND | ITALY | SPAIN | SWEDEN | UNITED KINGDOM

PE

AUSTRIA

I have always heard of the cobblestone streets throughout Austria that are filled with the sounds of local street performers playing classical music on their violins. Despite traveling through Europe many times, I never made it to Austria. Fortunately, I have many friends who travel as much as I do. One of them is my dear friend Cleo, and she was more than happy to share her experience in Austria for this book. Here's what she told me:

On a work trip to Vienna, Austria, in 2014, I was blown away by the beauty of the Volksgarten public park in the Innere Stadt first district of Vienna. The garden has just about 400 different types of roses and is part of the Hofburg Palace. I soon discovered the entire city was a culturally enriching experience. Such magnificent architecture, a beautiful juxtaposition of old and modern, the ancient castles, theaters and then there was the food...

Vienna is a meat lover's paradise, and the Wiener Schnitzel, or "Viennese cutlet" quickly became my favorite. Wiener Szchnitzel is a Viennese breaded pan-fried veal cutlet. I did a little research among the locals and the stories surrounding the origin are a little sketchy. Some say the recipe came from Italy to Vienna in 1857. Nevertheless, what I found out to be undeniably true is that the Schnitzel is one of the best-known specialties of Viennese cuisine, and one of the national dishes of Austria. And yes, I can attest, one of the tastiest dishes I enjoyed on my short stay.

I'll share a little secret: on my first attempt, I made the more popular variation using pork instead of veal, fried in refined coconut oil. Delicious! Please enjoy or as they say in German "Guten Appetit!"

VEAL SCHNITZEL

PREP
15-20 mins.

COOK
8 mins.

SKILL LEVEL
Medium

SERVES
4

EUROPE

INGREDIENTS

- 4-6 boneless veal or pork loin chops (chicken breast if desired, ½-inch thickness)
- ½ tsp. salt
- ½ tsp. garlic powder
- ½ tsp. white pepper
- ½ cup flour
- 1 cup dried bread crumbs
- 2 eggs, lightly beaten
- ¼ cup milk
- lard or butter, enough to just submerge cutlets (you may also substitute with refined coconut oil)

INSTRUCTIONS

Place cutlets between two sheets of waxed paper or plastic wrap. With a meat mallet or rolling pin, pound evenly to ⅛-inch thickness.

Sprinkle both sides of cutlets with salt.

In three separate bowls, place i) flour and garlic powder, ii) eggs and milk, iii) breadcrumbs. Lightly coat cutlets in flour, dip in egg mixture, then into breadcrumbs to coat.

Heat oil in a large nonstick skillet over medium-high heat.

Add cutlets to skillet; cook cutlets turning until golden brown for about 4 minutes per side.

Remove cutlets to a warm platter. Serve immediately with a traditional Austrian potato salad or mixed greens.

Chef's tip: To be honest, I know my version isn't the "traditional" way of making Schnitzel, but adding panko breadcrumbs gives it a really crispy texture. I personally love it like that. If you are a traditionalist, stick to the regular breadcrumbs. I make my own by just crushing up a piece of baguette and letting it sit out on the counter covered by a towel for 2-3 days. Baguettes are crunchy by nature, so it helps to make the Schnitzel crispier.

JEREMIAH KNIGHT

AUSTRIAN CUCUMBER SALAD

PREP
15 mins.

COOK
0

SKILL LEVEL
Easy

SERVES
3-4

INGREDIENTS

- 1 cucumber, thinly sliced
- salt, to taste
- 1 garlic clove, finely chopped
- 4 tbsp. grapeseed oil (or avocado oil)
- 4 tbsp. water
- 4 tbsp. vinegar
- 1 tbsp. lemon juice
- 1 tsp. sugar
- a pinch black pepper

INSTRUCTIONS

Wash and finely slice cucumber. Mix with salt and leave to stand for 10-15 minutes.

By hand, squeeze any liquid from the slices and pour away.

In a blender, mix grapeseed oil, garlic, sugar, water and lemon juice to create the marinade.

Mix cucumbers in marinade and add black pepper.

BELGIUM

I always said I wanted to visit Belgium during my studies in the United Kingdom. However, it was not until I was working in Southeast Asia that the opportunity arose to visit Brussels.

Walking through the cobblestoned streets of the central city transports you to a distant time when kings and queens ruled the land and lived in lofty castles. When touring the city, it became clear that besides the nation's fixation on beer, fish, and seafood, there was a clear love for all things chocolate. The level of artistry in the chocolate shops was astounding! My only problem is that... *I hate chocolate!* Yes, I said it, I do not like chocolate. Ever since I was a child, I never enjoyed the taste of it. However, I do appreciate white chocolate which in essence isn't really chocolate at all. So, when I went into these fine chocolate establishments requesting white chocolate, I would always get weird looks and pressure to purchase some high-level artisan dark chocolate instead.

The chocolate was lovely for what it was, but my favorite Belgian treat was a savory dish worth every bite. It was in a restaurant located in Grande-Place de Bruxelles where I had my first experience with a traditional presentation of *moules marinière* (mussels in a white wine sauce). This is one of the most popular dishes in the country, and I can see why! The fresh flavors of the mussels, married with a creamy white wine sauce provide the perfect base for dipping hot French fries, or a warm crusty bread.

Over the past years I have explored this dish with family and friends, searching for the perfect recipe. More important than the search for food perfection, were the soul-searching, wonderful stories shared by each person with whom I've cooked this dish. Each experience added a slightly different approach and captured a different version of the recipe. So now I share mine with you. Enjoy!

MOULES MARINIÈRE

PREP
15 mins.

COOK
3 mins.

SKILL LEVEL
Easy

SERVES
4

INGREDIENTS

- 4 lb. fresh mussels
- ¼ cup unsalted butter
- 3 shallots
- 4 oz. dry white wine
- 4 oz. heavy cream
- 2 bay leaves
- ½ bunch parsley
- 3-4 allspice berries
- 8 twigs thyme
- ½ tsp. crushed red pepper
- sea salt (to taste)
- white pepper (to taste)

EUROPE

INSTRUCTIONS

Chop up shallots and put them in a deep pot with butter and allspice berries. Saute until shallots become translucent.

Add white wine, herbs, and mussels, and cook for 4-5 minutes (or until they open).

Take out mussels and reserve in a covered bowl.

To the pot, add heavy cream, crushed red peppers, and white pepper.

Cook over medium heat until mixture slightly thickens (if needed, add ½ teaspoon of flour to thicken).

Return mussels to the pot and garnish with chopped parsley.

Serve with French fries.

Chef's tip: The allspice berries are my way of adding a Caribbean flair to this traditional dish. Remember that if the mussels do not open after being cooked, do not force them open, it means they are not fresh. **Throw them away!** Only eat the ones that naturally open on their own. Some people like to use cooking wine. It is too salty for me, and I prefer just using a nice wine you can find at your local grocery store. You don't have to use an expensive bottle. In this particular dish, a nice dry white wine (Chardonnay or a Sauvignon Blanc) will work perfectly. If you can't find shallots, then just use a nice sweet yellow onion.

BELGIAN WAFFLES

 PREP	 COOK	 SKILL LEVEL	 SERVES
15 mins.	0	Easy	3-4

INGREDIENTS

- **1¾ cups all-purpose flour**
- **3 tsp. baking powder**
- **½ tsp. salt**
- **2 large eggs, separated**
- **1¾ cups milk or dairy-free milk**
- **½ oil vegetable, canola, or melted coconut oil**

INSTRUCTIONS

Combine dry ingredients: In a large bowl, sift together flour, baking powder, and salt.

Separate the egg yolks and whites into two different mixing bowls. Be careful not to get any yellow egg yolk in with the egg whites. Use a hand mixer to beat the egg whites until they form stiff peaks.

Combine wet ingredients: In the bowl with the egg yolks, add the milk and oil, and mix. Stir in the dry ingredients.

Gently fold in egg whites, being careful not to over-mix.

Cook waffles: Spoon batter into preheated and greased waffle iron and cook according to waffle maker instructions.

Serve with syrup or your favorite toppings. Chef's suggestions: powdered sugar, Nutella, strawberry jam, berries, bananas, or whipped cream.

FRANCE

From Paris's decadent dishes to the sunbathed Mediterranean flavors of the Côte d'Azur, I found myself enchanted with all that the nation's gastronomy had to offer. Side alleys, main streets, plazas... you name it, all are filled with tempting culinary delights. After a few trips to the country, I was in awe of the diversity found within its regions. I vividly remember my first trip to the South of France where I was stunned by the light and fresh flavors of the Mediterranean – they were a beautiful contrast to the rich, creamy, and hearty flavors I was originally introduced to in the nation's capital. Everyone knows (or should know) how important food is to French culture and identity. However, you never fully gather an appreciation for it until you actually spend some time in the country. From the simple breakfast of *pain au chocolat* with a cup of coffee, to sitting down at a fine restaurant for dinner starting off with some amazing *foie gras*, your taste buds are left in a constant state of enchantment. But don't be intimidated by a nation's reputation for having exquisite cuisine. Instead, let your kitchen become a laboratory to experiment and perfect your mastery of it!

Every time I cook *fricassee de poulet* (chicken fricassee) I am reminded of my initial trip to France. France was the last stop of a whirlwind six-country European excursion I embarked upon during my college spring break while studying in London. By the time I arrived in Paris, I was completely broke and in search of good local food that was affordable! After stopping a number of Parisians on the street, it became clear that the Latin Quarter of Paris was the place to go to, not only to adhere to my budget, but also to provide a tantalizing introduction to French cuisine. I will never forget my first night dining in Paris. My two Morehouse College brothers and I made our way to the Latin Quarter and we discovered this small restaurant that had a set menu which sounded tasty and was affordable. It was there I experienced the recipe I am about to share. The main dish had a savory, creamy presentation of chicken accompanied with French fries and fresh greens.

This chicken dish reflects the true definition of comfort food. After years of experimenting with the recipe, I have created a unique version that incorporates various aspects of the French kitchen.

FRICASSEE DE POULET

PREP
30 mins.

COOK
1 hr.

SKILL LEVEL
Medium

SERVES
4

INGREDIENTS

- 8 boneless chicken thighs
- french grey salt or fine sea salt
- freshly ground pepper
- 3 tbsp. unsalted butter, softened, divided
- 1 tbsp. olive oil
- 1 cup shallots, diced fresh
- 8 oz. fresh mushrooms, trimmed, quartered
- 2 tbsp. all-purpose flour
- 1 cup dry white wine
- 2 cups chicken broth
- 3 tbsp. herbes de provence
- 1 bay leaf
- 3-4 tbsp. Dijon mustard (preferably with whole mustard seeds)
- ¼ cup heavy cream
- 2-3 tbsp. roughly chopped fresh tarragon leaves

EUROPE

INSTRUCTIONS

Preheat a deep-frying pan over medium heat and melt butter along with oil. Add chicken (skin side down) and fry until golden brown (about 5 minutes on each side). Do not overcrowd pan with chicken! The pieces need space in order to remain crispy and golden.

Remove chicken from the pan. Reduce the heat, and add shallots and fresh tarragon, and cook until shallots become translucent.

Add mushrooms and cook until soft.

Add white wine and bring to a boil.

Mix flour and chicken broth together. Lower heat, add the mixture to the pan and stir constantly. Once thickened, slowly add heavy cream.

Place chicken in a large oven dish and pour cream sauce on top. Place in the oven and cook for 10-15 minutes.

Garnish with additional tarragon.

Chef's tip: You may need to clean the pan a few times while frying the chicken in butter. Don't wait until the bottom starts to burn. When you see a significant build up, remove the residue and place it aside. You will need it because it adds wonderful flavor to the sauce. Clean the pan and start again. You may need to repeat this step more than once.

FRENCH CARROT SALAD

PREP
15 mins.

COOK
0

SKILL LEVEL
Easy

SERVES
4-5

INGREDIENTS

- 1 pound carrots, peeled, julienned (approximately 5-6 medium size ones)
- 3 tsp. Dijon mustard
- 1 tbsp. freshly squeezed lemon juice
- 2 tbsp. grapeseed oil
- 2 tbsp. extra virgin olive oil
- 2 tsp. honey
- ½ tsp. salt
- ½ tsp. freshly ground white pepper
- 3 tbsp. chervil
- 1 finely chopped shallot

INSTRUCTIONS

In a salad bowl, combine the Dijon mustard, lemon juice, honey, grapeseed oil, olive oil, salt and pepper. Add the carrots, chervil and shallots, and toss well. Taste and adjust seasoning if necessary. Cover and refrigerate until ready to serve.

ICELAND

Everyone who is hip and cool now knows that Iceland is off da chain! (Are the kids still saying that?) Iceland is one of the places people visit to feel "trendy" and "adventurous." However, long before Iceland became a place to flaunt one's status on social media, I developed an inexplicable infatuation with the island.

My very first memories of Iceland came from Encyclopedia Britannica and an article I read in National Geographic as a child. For some reason, this island nation, situated in the most northern region of the world, provided the right level of uniqueness to keep my young mind intrigued about its people and, of course, its food. So, when my home economics teacher (*remember when that was a high school requirement?*) asked the class to pick a country to cook from and present to our classmates, of course I decided that I wanted to learn how to make Icelandic food.

I will never forget the day of the culinary presentations. Each student presented their cultural findings and the teacher then provided them with a recipe from their nation to prepare. Italy, Jamaica, and France were a few of the obvious choices presented. After I finished my Icelandic presentation (which by the way, I personally thought was the best out of them all!) my teacher handed me a recipe for ... *Swedish meatballs*?

I was a bit confused. I love Swedish meatballs, but I did not want to cook Swedish food, I wanted to cook Icelandic food! Right away, I went up to my teacher and asked why I was handed a recipe from Sweden. Her response was that it was almost impossible to find an Icelandic recipe, so it was just easier to cook the one she shared. I never forgot that day and decided that one day I would have the opportunity to taste Icelandic cuisine.

Many years later, in the summer of 2012, I was in my office searching for flights when I discovered a really inexpensive flight from New York City to Reykjavik (Iceland's capital). I immediately called my dear travel adventure friend Neda and we set out together in search of authentic, traditional, delicious Icelandic food.

Iceland's food, people, geography and even its nightlife (despite 24-hour summer sun) outstripped my expectations. I love how the Icelandic people seemed to be so in-tune with nature and devoted to creating a "green" society. Fresh spring water is piped right into their homes; they use natural heat from geothermal springs; they have carbon-free power generation; they even fish and hunt in a sustainable way. The country is a global model of how to live in harmony with nature in the modern world.

The people there are also extremely friendly. I met a group of Icelanders at a reception while in Reykjavik. By the end of the reception, they invited me to go partying with them, and I did not return to my hotel until 7 o'clock the next morning!

ICELANDIC JUNIPER-CURED SALMON

PREP
30 mins.

CURE
3 days

SKILL LEVEL
Easy

SERVES
8-10

EUROPE

As soon as I returned to the United States, I went online and ordered an Icelandic cookbook. The juniper-cured salmon recipe I share in this book is my take on a traditional Icelandic dish. It is a standard when I try to introduce people to Scandinavian cuisine. It is relatively simple, but some of the best tasting dishes are often the ones that are the easiest to prepare. The key is to use the freshest salmon you can find.

INGREDIENTS

- 2 lb. fresh salmon fillet
- 5 tsp. coarse sea salt
- 3 tsp. brown sugar
- 12 juniper berries, crushed
- 10 white peppercorns
- 4-5 sprigs fresh dill

INSTRUCTIONS

Mix all the ingredients and cover the salmon completely with the mix on both sides.

Place the seasoned salmon in an airtight sealed plastic bag.

Place in the refrigerator for three days.

Twice daily, turn the salmon onto the opposite side.

On the third day, remove salmon from the plastic bag and lightly dust off the mix of ingredients.

Thinly slice the salmon after dusting the ingredients off and serve with toasted rye bread.

Hot Versions:
After the salmon has cured for 3 days, sear it in a frying pan with butter. 3-5 mins on each side. You can serve it on a bed of watercress.

Chef's tip: I know I provided a "hot" option for the recipe, but the original cold version tastes so amazing. By the third day, it will be cured so don't worry about eating raw fish if that is what scares you. Either way, be sure to brush off the fish completely before the last phase of the preparation.

JEREMIAH KNIGHT

PIPARKÖKUR

PREP
30 mins.

COOK
7-9 mins.

SKILL LEVEL
Medium

SERVES
2 dozen

EUROPE

I didn't actually discover these addictive holiday cookies during my Icelandic adventures. Instead, I was relaxing on my porch in South Sudan 5 years after my trip to Iceland trying to find out what I could make for the embassy's Christmas party. I wanted something I could include in my annual holiday meals that would stand out on its own. Because the Nordic region is internationally renowned for being the land of Santa Claus and Christmas spirit, I decided to take a look at what Iceland had to offer for Christmas desserts. After checking out a number of blogs and websites, I kept seeing recipes for *Piparkokur* (Icelandic Pepper Cookies) which are typical for Christmas. I decided to try out two dozen of them for the Christmas party at the Ambassador's home. The cookies came out exceptional and were a hit at the party. Since then, they have become the Christmas cookie that I share with friends and family. Here is my take on a quintessential Icelandic Christmas cookie!

INGREDIENTS

- **2 cups flour**
- **2 cups brown sugar**
- **2 sticks (8 oz.) unsalted softened butter**
- **2 eggs**
- **2 tsp. baking powder**
- **1 tsp. baking soda**
- **2 tsp. powdered ginger**
- **1 tsp. cinnamon**
- **½ tsp. powdered cloves**
- **¼ tsp. ground black pepper**
- **¼ tsp. ground white pepper**
- **¼ tsp. paprika**
- **¼ tsp. allspice**

INSTRUCTIONS

Preset oven to 390⁰ F.

Adding the period at end for consistency.

Mix the dry ingredients.

Add soft butter and eggs, and knead until smooth.

Place mixture into plastic wrap and roll into two long sausage shapes.

Place in the refrigerator overnight.

Cut dough rolls into thin slices about ⅕ of an inch (5mm) in thickness.

Put slices on a cookie sheet covered with baking paper (or greased and floured surface).

Bake until golden brown, about 7-9 mins.

ITALY

My first views of Rome – flying over the ancient city as my plane prepared for landing – will never be forgotten. It was the beginning of a three-week spring break trip across Europe with three college friends that will forever be etched in my mind.

But of course, over the six days I then spent in Italy, what really stood out to me – the thing I really could never forget – was the food. I appreciated how Italians allow fresh pastas to be dressed by light sauces. They were not drenched in sauce, something I had become accustomed to growing up in America. I also marveled at how Italians seem to always make time to truly relax and have a meal. It doesn't matter how much hustle and bustle is going on in the streets, when you walk into a restaurant, things magically slow down and people take their time to enjoy their meals.

My dear friend Keyla, who was with me in Italy, enjoyed her time there as much as I did. When I spoke to her about this book, she made me promise to give her space to share one of her culinary journeys. She then got upset with me because I told her that she could only include one recipe in the book. She wanted to have both sweet and savory dishes included.

I couldn't keep a good friend mad at me, so I gave in. The first recipe, for the traditional Italian dessert Tiramisu, is from Keyla, who later told me its name means, "Lift Me Up."

"I just knew I had to try to recreate this dish and the feeling of happiness it inspired," she said.

TIRAMISU

PREP
30 mins.

COOK
1 hr.

SKILL LEVEL
Medium

SERVES
4

INGREDIENTS

- 6 large eggs
- ½ cup sugar or a small can of condensed milk
- 16 oz. mascarpone cheese
- 2 oz. Kahlúa or dark rum
- 1 oz. amaretto
- 12-14 ladyfingers
- 1½ cups brewed espresso coffee
- ½ cup sliced almonds
- 1 tbsp. powdered nutmeg
- powdered cinnamon
- 2 tbsp. coconut oil
- unsweetened cocoa powder, for garnish

EUROPE

INSTRUCTIONS

Set aside 3 tablespoons of sugar or ¼ cup condensed milk for later.

Separate egg yolks from egg whites.

In a clean bowl, using a hand mixer, whip the egg whites and sugar or condensed milk (except for the reserves) together with a hand mixer, until the egg whites form stiff peaks.

In a separate bowl, whip the egg yolks with the remaining sugar or condensed milk for 2-3 minutes until the egg yolks are thick and pale yellow.

Slightly toast almond slices in coconut oil until golden brown.

Mix the mascarpone cheese with the toasted almonds.

Add the mascarpone mix to the egg yolks and whip until combined. Fold egg whites into the egg yolk mixture and set aside.

In a separate bowl, combine the espresso and amaretto. Soak each ladyfinger into the espresso mixture and place them in rows in the bottom of a serving pan or dish.

Spread half of the mascarpone mixture over the ladyfingers.

Arrange another layer of espresso-soaked ladyfingers and spread the remaining mascarpone cream on top.

Mix the cocoa powder with a pinch of nutmeg and cinnamon. Use a sifter or colander to sprinkle mixture over the dish.

Cover the dish and refrigerate for 2-4 hours before serving. Enjoy the deliciousness.

CACIO E PEPE PASTA

PREP
25 mins.

COOK
20 mins.

SKILL LEVEL
Easy

SERVES
3

INGREDIENTS

- 6 oz. pasta of choice (preferably spaghetti or angel hair pasta)
- 3 tbsp. butter, softened
- 1-2 tsp. fresh black and red pepper
- ¾ cup finely grated Grana Padano or parmesan cheese
- ⅓ cup finely grated pecorino
- ½ cup ripe cherry or grape tomatoes (optional)
- 1 tsp. fresh minced garlic
- ¼ cup fresh parsley
- 2 sage leaves
- olive oil to taste

INSTRUCTIONS

Cook pasta as you normally would, adding a bit of salt to the water as it boils.

Remove from heat, drain and reserve.

In a saucepan melt 2 tablespoons of butter; add pepper and garlic until toasted.

Add the tomatoes and sage, reduce to low heat.

After 2 minutes add Grana Padano or parmesan cheese, stirring and tossing with tongs until melted.

Turn off the heat; pour the sauce on the pasta until fully coated. Serve and sprinkle parsley and olive oil to garnish.

Chef's tip: For the Cacio e Pepe Pasta, purchase fresh pasta and not the dry one. If you can't find any at the store, go online and get a simple recipe for making pasta. It will make a world of difference with the dish. Also, don't be cheap on the cheese. Buy some good cheese please!

SPAIN

When I first visited Spain years ago, I was a university student, and – like so many young and inexperienced people do – I ended up finding myself at only touristy locations. Six years later I returned, determined to focus on where my taste buds could lead me.

That led me to a tortilla Española, which I experienced for the first time at a local friend's home in Barcelona. A tortilla Española is one of many tapas – or appetizers – but tapas are more than mere appetizers. They are a complete experience. Wine, bread, cheese, olives, small savory bites – they all come together with great conversation to create a lifetime of memories. The simple but tasty tortilla Española captured my attention, and I immediately launched a full-scale investigation into making it.

During this second stay in Spain, I made a point of trying as many versions of the dish as I could in order to determine how to incorporate it into my own kitchen. I then spent the next six years attempting to recreate what I experienced.

Years later, while living in the Dominican Republic, I was invited to the house of my dear friend Yadira for a Christmas party. Her Spanish neighbor Ana (also a friend of mine) arrived with two tortillas Española. Ana's tortilla was rich in flavor, with perfect texture and color – it immediately transported me to my first experience with the dish years prior in Barcelona. During the remainder of my time in the Dominican Republic, Christmas could not be complete without tortillas Española, Ana style!

When I told Ana I was preparing this book, I asked if I could include her recipe. She responded with an enthusiastic, "Yes!" This recipe is dedicated to my dear friend Ana. Thanks for allowing me to share a little part of Spain with the world.

ANA'S TORTILLA ESPAÑOLA

PREP
30 mins.

COOK
50 mins.

SKILL LEVEL
Medium

SERVES
8-10

Always served with a slice of fresh bread, tortilla Española can be eaten at any time of day. With a nice simple salad of fresh greens and cherry tomatoes, you have a perfect meal.

INGREDIENTS

- **2 lb. potatoes, thinly sliced**
- **2 large onions, diced**
- **salt and pepper (to taste)**
- **1 large, sweet bell pepper, diced**
- **5-6 large eggs**
- **1 tsp. paprika**

EUROPE

INSTRUCTIONS

In a large, nonstick skillet with a generous amount of virgin olive oil, fry potatoes, onions and bell peppers with spices.

Beat eggs until light and fluffy.

Remove from heat and add the beaten eggs.

Use another clean large nonstick skillet to heat a tablespoon of olive oil over medium heat.

Add potato-egg mixture.

Every minute or so gently shuffle to avoid sticking.

When the bottom has turned golden brown, remove the skillet from the stove, place the tortilla on a large plate, turn it over and place the undone side face-down in the skillet.

Again, every minute or so gently shuffle to avoid sticking. When the face-down side is golden brown (make sure the center is a bit soft), remove from the skillet and place on a large serving platter. You can garnish with parsley or chives.

Chef's tip: **The perfect tortilla has to be a bit soft on the inside. It can't be 100% cooked. Use a nonstick pan so it's easier to turn it over. Also, a well-greased cast iron pan will work if you do not have a nonstick pan.**

PASSION FRUIT SANGRIA

PREP
1 hr.

COOK
0

SKILL LEVEL
Easy

SERVES
4-6

EUROPE

During my numerous visits to Spain, I always found myself with friends at outdoor cafes, snacking on tapas and quenching our thirst with sangrias. The red sangrias are the most traditional, and they embody all that speaks of Spain. They use traditional red Spanish wines which are a perfect accompaniment to the tapas that are served with them. Being the Caribbean soul I am, I wanted to capture the heart of this refreshing drink but also include tropical flavors to bring it to new shores. Here is my take on this quintessential Spanish drink.

INGREDIENTS

- 1 bottle red wine (preferably a dry hearty one)
- ½ cup brandy
- ½ cup simple brown sugar syrup (recipe below) or substitute for honey
- ⅓ cup St. Germain or any elderflower liqueur
- ¼ cup Cointreau liqueur
- ½ cup fresh passion fruit pulp
- ½ cup cut mango
- 1 orange, peeled and diced
- 1 star fruit, sliced
- 2 limes

INSTRUCTIONS

In a large vase, add diced orange, mango, simple syrup, St. Germaine, Cointreau, brandy and the juice of one lime.

Slice the other lime and add to the mixture.

Fill the vase with the wine, mix with a wooden spoon and let it chill for at least an hour.

Serve on ice.

SIMPLE BROWN SUGAR SYRUP

INGREDIENTS:

- 3 cups water
- 3 cups brown sugar

INSTRUCTIONS

Heat water in a saucepan, but avoid boiling.

Mix in brown sugar and continue to stir until all sugar is dissolved.

Once dissolved, remove from heat and let cool. Store excess simple syrup in the refrigerator in a sealable container.

SWEDEN

I am so in love with Scandinavian culinary culture! The unembellished, pure, and natural approach to how the countries of the region design their meals always brings a smile to my face. I have not extensively traveled through the region so thanks to my friend Claudia, I am able to share in her culinary travels there.

I met Claudia in 2012 while working in Washington, D.C. We worked in the same office and developed a friendship that was definitely strengthened by our mutual love of food, and in particular desserts. We both have a sweet tooth. However, the recipe she has shared for this book is not a dessert. I believe this is her attempt to mask what she really wants. But do not be mistaken, this savory recipe rocks and needs to be included in this book!

Claudia, thanks for the story and recipe. No judgment from my end! I will always love you and be your friend, no matter how hard you try to cover up the fact that you struggle with sweets! This one is for you Claudia.

Claudia writes:

"I'm a sucker for dessert. Of every kind, flavor, texture - you name it and I'll eat it. When my husband, Andrew, and I traveled to Sweden to celebrate our first wedding anniversary in September 2015, we made sure to do so with the top tier of our wedding cake by our side.

I was amazed at how much the Swedes embraced their dessert. People actually ate cake for breakfast!

As we walked along the charming streets, tired from eating so much sugar and still a bit jet-lagged from the day before, we came across a small restaurant that had a very homey feel to it. We took a gander, spotted a couple of plates and then decided this spot was legit. I was too tired to look it up on Yelp and too hungry to walk any further, so I gave in. We were seated immediately by the window - a romantic scene in sight. We knew Sweden was known for its meatballs so we each ordered a plate.

This dish was one of the best dishes of our lives. Albeit simple, each bite was divine and packed with myriad flavors. The meatballs were cooked to perfection. The gravy was out of this world. We both inhaled the dish and came back the next day for seconds. When we got back to our hotel and sliced into our cake, we found ourselves disappointed; we actually didn't care for dessert at that moment and continued to rave about the meatballs!"

Claudia, thanks for making your story part of my culinary adventures!

AMOROSA

SWEDISH MEATBALLS

PREP
30 mins.

COOK
25-30 mins.

SKILL LEVEL
Medium

SERVES
4-5

INGREDIENTS

Meatballs:
- ½ lb. ground pork
- ½ lb. ground beef
- ¼ cup panko bread crumbs
- ¼ tsp. ground allspice
- ¼ tsp. ground nutmeg
- ¼ cup onion, finely chopped
- 2 cloves garlic, chopped
- ⅛ tsp. pepper
- ½ tsp. salt
- 1 egg
- 1 tbsp. olive oil
- 2 tbsp. butter

Meatball gravy:
- 2 tbsp. butter
- 3 tbsp. flour
- 1 cup heavy cream
- 2 cups beef broth
- 1 tbsp. Worcestershire sauce
- salt and pepper to taste

EUROPE

INSTRUCTIONS

In a large bowl, combine ground pork, ground beef, panko bread crumbs, allspice, nutmeg, onion, garlic, egg, salt and pepper.

Mix until combined, then roll into 20 meatballs (1.5 inches each).

In a large skillet, heat olive oil and butter (medium to high heat, but be careful - nobody likes burnt butter!)

Add meatballs, and continue turning them until brown on each side and cooked throughout (8-10 minutes).

Remove the meatballs from the skillet and drain on a plate lined with paper towels.

Cover with foil.

For meatball gravy
Reduce heat, then add butter and flour to the same skillet and whisk until browned.

Slowly stir in beef broth and heavy cream. Add Worcestershire sauce and bring to a simmer until sauce starts to thicken.

Add salt and pepper to taste.

Add the meatballs to the skillet and simmer for 10 minutes at a low heat.

Last but not least, serve over mashed potatoes and pair with lingonberry jam!

RAGGMUNK

PREP
40-45 mins.

COOK
20 mins.

SKILL LEVEL
Medium

SERVES
4-5

INGREDIENTS

- 1½ cups whole milk
- ½ cup heavy cream
- ¾ cup flour
- 2 tsp. sea salt
- 1 large egg
- 1¾ lb. potatoes
- a dash of allspice
- butter for frying

INSTRUCTIONS

Mix milk, heavy cream and flour in a bowl.

Add egg and salt, and mix.

Use a fine grater to grate potatoes. Then add them to the batter.

Allow batter to rest for at least 35 minutes.

Melt butter in a frying pan and pour in about ½ cup of the batter. Fry at medium heat until both sides are golden brown and crispy.

Serve with your favorite berry jam/preserve.

TURKEY

Turkey is a geographical, cultural, and gastronomic bridge between Europe and Asia. Over the centuries, the two continents have flawlessly merged to create the vibrant and distinct Turkish culture we know. During one of my many trips to Turkey I became addicted to the flaky perfection of a good baklava. I was hooked on it by a small bakery, tucked away on a busy street in one of Istanbul's oldest neighborhoods. My friends and I stopped there every evening during that trip. We would sit outside, sip tea and watch the sunset while treating ourselves to endless servings of baklava – life doesn't get any sweeter! On our final night in Istanbul, we visited the bakery one last time, and before we said goodbye the owners brought us behind the counter to get a closer look at the artistry of their pastry chefs. He gave us a tour of where the magic happened. From the area where the flakey pastry was created, the vat of fragrant syrup, to the section that was used to prepare the filling, it told a story of his family's role in preserving Turkey's culinary history.

Turkish people are extremely proud. I often think about the meal my friends and I had in the town of Cappadocia. We went into this small, traditional restaurant where we sat comfortably on the floor and experienced even more of that famous Turkish hospitality. We ate so much that we *literally slept right there at the table* for at least 45 minutes post meal! No one rushed us away; instead, they smiled and joked with us, understanding that we really enjoyed what we had just experienced. And we sure did!

There are many versions of baklava and, believe me, I think I tried almost all of them during my time in Turkey. However, the lighter and more delicate properties of *sutlu nuriye* caused it to become my muse for *Diplomat In The Kitchen* - I picked this one because it's similar to the popular baklava, but with an easier approach. I hope you enjoy it!

SUTLU NURIYE

PREP
30-40 mins.

COOK
30-45 mins.

SKILL LEVEL
Medium-Hard

SERVES
30

INGREDIENTS

- 12 filo sheets (each sheet 480 mm x 255 mm)
- 1 cup (approximate) unsalted melted butter
- 12 oz. hazelnuts, chopped/crushed

For the syrup:
- 2 cups water
- 1 ½ cups whole milk
- 1 cup brown sugar
- ⅓ cup honey
- 2 green cardamom pods
- ½ tsp. rosewater essence (optional)

INSTRUCTIONS

Grease the baking dish with some of the melted butter.

Place two more filo pastry sheets on top and brush with melted butter.

Place another two sheets over them and brush with melted butter.

Crush the hazelnuts either by using a food processor, pulsing only a few times, or by chopping them by hand.

Spread the chopped hazelnuts evenly on the sixth sheet of buttered filo pastry.

Lay two more sheets of filo pastry and brush with melted butter. Repeat this two more times, buttering every two sheets, until you have placed the twelfth sheet.

Brush the twelfth sheet of filo pastry with butter and ease the sheets into the corners of the baking dish, trimming the edges if necessary.

Then, using a sharp knife, cut through all the layers to form 30 small square pieces.

Put the sugar into a heavy pan, pour in water and cardamom pods, and bring to a boil, stirring all the time. Once the sugar is dissolved, lower the heat and simmer for 10 minutes.

Pour the milk into the pan, give a good stir and turn the heat off. Place the pan aside and leave to cool down; once cool, remove the cardamom pods. (Heads up: The syrup will need to be lukewarm to pour over the pastry, so you will have to reheat the syrup when the pastry is almost ready to take out of the oven.)

Once the filo pastry is cooked and golden on the top, take it out of the oven and let it cool for approximately 15 minutes.

When cool, slowly pour lukewarm milky syrup over the pastry and let it soak through for 35-40 minutes.

Chef's tip: It is extremely important that you monitor the pastry while it is in the oven. You want it to be just turning golden. If you see that it is browning too fast, lower the heat a bit. Also, slab on the butter. The more you use, the flakier and tastier it will be.

MERCIMEK ÇORBASI

PREP
30-40 mins.

COOK
30-40 mins.

SKILL LEVEL
Medium

SERVES
4

INGREDIENTS

- 1½ tbsp. olive oil
- 1 yellow onion
- 3 cloves of garlic
- 1 medium sized carrot
- 1 large Irish potato
- 1½ cups red lentils, well washed
- 6 cups broth (vegetable, chicken or beef)
- ½ tsp. white pepper, freshly ground
- 1½ tbsp. tomato paste
- ½ tsp. sumac
- 1 lime (juice)
- ½ tsp. of red pepper flakes
- 2 tbsp. butter
- sprinkle of fresh chopped cilantro for garnish

INSTRUCTIONS

In a large soup pot, heat olive oil over medium-low heat in a large soup pot and add onion, carrot, and potato. Continue to stir them until they soften.

Add lentils, broth, tomato paste and white pepper. Bring the mixture to a boil and then reduce to a simmer. Cook for about 20-25 minutes or until lentils are falling apart.

Place mixture in a blender and blend until smooth.

Return mixture to the pot and add salt to taste if needed.

Add in sumac and butter, then simmer for 2-4 minutes.

Remove from heat, add in lime juice and red pepper flakes.

UNITED KINGDOM

The U.K. will always hold a special place in my heart. It was the first country that I ever lived in outside of the United States. My first experience with the British Isles began when I studied at the University of Westminster. Though I was far from home, it's a culture I easily adapted to. Plus, I have a fairly large extended British family that helped me adjust to my new surroundings. On weekends I would escape the university dormitories and invite friends to accompany me for Sunday dinner at my relatives' homes.

The most special Sunday dinner was always at the home of my Uncle Lynn. A retired master chef, Uncle Lynn relished the opportunity to host dinner parties. Dinners at his house were always highly sought after by relatives and friends, who wanted to experience the vibrant history of his culinary travels spanning the globe over 60 years. Never modest regarding his abilities, Uncle Lynn constantly challenged me to expand my culinary horizons by experimenting with new spices, recipes and techniques. The first time I ever ate English roasted potatoes – a common dish in the U.K. – was in his home. Of course, never one to be ordinary, he put a special twist on it. Every time I cook English-style roasted potatoes, I think of those Sunday adventures at the home of my dear Uncle Lynn. English-style roasted potatoes are a great accompaniment to almost any main course. He would have been proud to know that I too have placed my own flair on his version of this quintessential English dish.

For centuries, British cuisine has integrated other world cuisines into its national identity, always adding a twist of its own. I love that idea of fusion and often use the technique when I am preparing meals for friends and family.

While writing this book my dear Uncle Lynn passed away. I dedicate this one to you, Uncle. I know you are smiling down on me!

UNCLE LYNN'S ENGLISH ROASTED POTATOES

PREP
15-20 mins.

COOK
40-50 mins.

SKILL LEVEL
Easy

SERVES
4

INGREDIENTS

- 6 large potatoes
- 1 tbsp. sea salt
- 1 tbsp. pepper
- 1 tbsp. onion powder
- 1 tsp. paprika
- ¼ cup olive oil
- ½ cup melted unsalted butter
- ¼ cup chopped parsley
- ¼ cup of fresh chives

INSTRUCTIONS

Peel and quarter potatoes (you can leave the skins on for a heartier taste).

Chop them in quarters.

Place in a pot with water.

Bring to a boil and simmer for 5-6 minutes to slightly soften.

Meanwhile, preheat your oven to 400° F.

When the potatoes have simmered, drain them thoroughly in a colander, shaking to roughen edges.

Let sit for a few minutes to dry.

In a large bowl, mix melted butter, olive oil, salt, pepper, onion powder, and paprika.

Gently place potatoes in mixture and coat them with it evenly.

Turn potatoes once or twice (no more) halfway through (after 20 minutes or so) to ensure even cooking.

Cook in total for approximately 40-50 minutes until gold and crispy (observe closely once near end).

Garnish with parsley and chives.

Chef's tip: Do not boil the potatoes until they are completely cooked. Remember you will have to roast them after you boil them; you don't want them overdone. If you can come across some duck fat, use it rather than butter. It's not the healthiest option, but it sure does taste good. For those who wish to be a bit healthier only use olive oil.

EUROPE

JEREMIAH KNIGHT

YORKSHIRE PUDDING

PREP
10 mins.

COOK
20 mins.

SKILL LEVEL
Easy

SERVES
6

INGREDIENTS

- 4 large eggs
- ¾ cup whole milk
- ¼ cup half & half
- 1 cup flour
- a pinch of salt
- 2 tbsp. butter (to be authentic, use lard or drippings from roasted beef or chicken)

INSTRUCTIONS

Preheat oven to 400° F.

Pour the eggs and milk into a large mixing bowl and add a pinch of salt. Whisk thoroughly with an electric hand beater or hand whisk. Let stand for 10 minutes.

Gradually sieve the flour into the milk and egg mixture, again using an electric hand beater or hand whisk until completely smooth. Allow batter to rest for a minimum of 30 minutes.

Divide the butter evenly into the twelve cups of a muffin tin, about ½ teaspoon per cup. Place tin in oven to melt butter, 2 to 5 minutes. Remove from the oven.

Give the batter another good whisk, adding 2 tablespoons of cold water.

Fill one-third of each section of the tin with batter and return quickly to the oven.

Bake in the preheated oven for 5 minutes. Reduce heat to 350° F and bake 10-15 minutes more or until puffed and golden.

Trafalgar Square
Lambeth Bridge

NORTH AMERICA & THE CARIBB

CANADA | UNITED STATES | DOMINICAN REPUBLIC | MEXICO | JAMAICA | BAHAMAS

EAN

CANADA

To me, Canada is like the cousin that you haven't seen for years, but when you finally see her at a family gathering, it's nothing but laughter, love, and pure good times! Friendly and inviting culture has been a hallmark of Canada; the people are known to provide visitors easy access to all the beauty it has to offer. But Canada, to me, is not only a metaphorical distant cousin – it's also actually the home to many dear cousins and other family members whom I know I should visit much more often.

During my first trip, I started off right away inquiring about "true" Canadian cuisine. Like its neighbor to the south, Canada's culinary identity is one that over centuries has woven strong Indigenous elements into the fare of the immigrants who made their way to its shores. I found Canada's food to be rich and diverse with some striking similarities to American cuisine.

After a couple days of exploring the city's restaurant scene, my cousin insisted that I could not leave Canada without tasting *poutine*, (the classic Canadian dish of French fries smothered in gravy and cheese curd. Poutine is enjoyed in all regions of the country, but it was invented in Quebec in the 1950s. The key elements are simple, hardy, and comforting, proving that you don't always have to fly to distant lands to discover culinary treasures; sometimes they may be much closer than you think!

The first time I tried poutine was around midnight after spending a night out on the town. Me being the purist that I am (not really!) I opted for my first experience with poutine to be the traditional version which consists of French fries, cheese curd and gravy. I know it's not my usual move, but I'm glad I went traditional. *Just amazing!* It was the perfect answer to a midnight craving. However, this dish is not only to be shared in the midnight after-party hours. It should also be celebrated at brunches and lunches (and everything in between). Here is my take on this must-have Canadian dish!

CANADIAN POUTINE

PREP
1 hr.

COOK
30 mins.

SKILL LEVEL
Medium

SERVES
3

INGREDIENTS

Poutine Gravy:
- 3 tbsp. cornstarch
- 6 tbsp. unsalted butter
- ¼ cup unbleached all-purpose flour
- 2 cloves garlic
- 1 shallot, finely chopped
- a pinch black pepper
- 20 oz. beef broth (chicken broth can be used as a substitute)

Deep Fried Fries:
- 2 lb. Russet potatoes (3-4 medium potatoes)
- cooking oil

Toppings:
- 1-1½ cups white cheddar cheese curds (torn chunks of fresh mozzarella cheese would be the closest substitute)
- ¼ cup finely chopped parsley and chives

INSTRUCTIONS

Peel the potatoes and cut them into ½ inch thick slices. Place them in a large bowl. Cover with cold water and refrigerate for an hour.

In a frying pan, sauté the shallot and garlic until golden brown (reserve them).

In a large saucepan, melt the butter over a medium heat. Add the flour and cook, stirring regularly, for about 5 minutes, until the mixture turns golden brown.

Add broth and bring to a boil, stirring with a whisk. Stir in the cornstarch (already dissolved in water) and shallot/garlic mixture.

Bring to a simmer for 3 to 5 minutes or until the sauce thickens. Season with pepper.

Deep fry the potatoes at 250° F for 3-4 minutes. Remove potatoes and place on paper towels to absorb excess oil. After they are set aside for 5-10 minutes, deep fry at 330° F until golden brown. Remove then lightly salt them.

Place hot fries in a shallow bowl, top with cheese curds followed by a generous ladle of thick gravy.

Add parsley and/or chive topping as garnish.

Chef's tip: Cheese curd really makes this dish. I know it is hard to find, but it's worth the trouble. I would suggest making some on your own, but it is a bit labor intensive. If you don't have cheese curd, get the best soft mozzarella or any other really soft cheese that has a light flavor.

BUTTER TART

PREP
20 mins.

COOK
15 mins.

SKILL LEVEL
Medium

SERVES
12

INGREDIENTS

Pastry crust:
- 1½ cups all-purpose flour
- ¼ tsp. salt
- ½ cup cold butter, cubed
- 1 large egg yolk
- 1 tbsp. fresh lemon juice
- Ice cold water

Filling:
- ½ cup dark brown sugar
- ½ cup honey
- 1 large, room-temperature egg
- 2 tbsp. very soft butter
- 1 tsp. vanilla extract
- 1 tsp. fresh lemon juice
- ½ tsp. lemon zest
- a pinch salt
- ⅓ cup mixed raisins and chopped walnuts

Powder:
- ¼ cup powdered sugar
- 1 tsp. nutmeg

INSTRUCTIONS

Preheat oven to 450 °F.

In a large bowl, mix flour and salt. With a pastry blender or manually, cut in the butter until the mixture resembles very fine crumbs.

In an 8-ounce measuring cup, use a fork to combine the egg yolk, lemon juice and enough iced water to come to ⅓ cup.

Gradually drizzle over the flour mixture, stirring briskly with a fork until the pastry holds together. You may need to add a little more iced water to gather up the last of the dry bits.

Press dough into a disc, and wrap and chill until firm. (But before rolling, let stand at room temperature to soften a little).

In a medium bowl, mix the sugar, honey, egg, butter, vanilla, lemon juice, zest and salt until smooth.

On a floured surface, roll out pastry to ⅛-inch thickness. Using a 4-inch round cookie cutter, cut out 12 circles, re-rolling scraps if necessary. Fit into muffin cups. Divide the raisin-walnut mixture among the pastry shells. Spoon the filling into the pastry shells until they are three-quarters full.

Bake in the bottom third of the oven for about 12 minutes, or until filling is puffed and bubbly, and the pastry is golden.

Let stand on a rack for one minute; then immediately run a metal spatula around tarts to loosen. Carefully slide the spatula under the tarts and lift out to cool on a rack.

Dust with powdered sugar and nutmeg.

UNITED STATES

It seems as though the older I get, the more I fall in love with the New England kitchen. Growing up in Connecticut, I didn't realize that a lot of what I was eating had its roots in the rich history and traditions of New England. To me, making homemade corn chowder, or going to our backyard to pick apples for apple pies, was just part of what every child did with their grandmother.

I had no idea how blessed I was to call New England home when I was younger. The fresh offerings of the sea, locally-grown berries and other produce, and hearty stews had somehow been effortlessly incorporated into the Caribbean and southern American parts of my life and my early culinary experiences. In particular, I always remember my grandmother having a cookbook titled, "Connecticut a la Carte."

About five years ago I asked my grandmother if I could have the book. Without thinking twice, she responded with a chuckle and an emphatic, "Yes!" The cookbook is now out of print and I don't know of any other traditional Connecticut cookbook, so it has now become a prized possession in my library. Within the book is a recipe that is quintessentially New England: New England Indian Pudding!

Over the past few years it has made a surprising resurgence on the menus of some of the region's award-winning restaurants. And now I share with you pieces of my homeland, and of the cookbook my grandmother allowed me to keep.

NEW ENGLAND INDIAN PUDDING

10-15 mins.

COOK
3+ hours

SKILL LEVEL
Medium

SERVES
8-10

INGREDIENTS

- 4 cups whole milk
- ½ cup stone-ground yellow cornmeal
- ⅔ cup firmly packed brown sugar
- 2 tbsp. unsalted butter
- 1 tsp. sea salt
- ½ tsp. freshly grated nutmeg
- ½ tsp. allspice
- ½ tsp. ginger
- ½ tsp. cinnamon
- ½ tsp. mace
- 2 large eggs
- 1 cup heavy cream

INSTRUCTIONS

Preheat oven to 300° F.

Scald 3 cups of milk.

Mix 1 cup cold milk with cornmeal; pour cornmeal mixture slowly into hot milk. Cook mixture for 25-30 minutes over low heat with constant stirring.

Add sugar, butter, molasses, then remove from heat. Add salt and spices; stir in beaten eggs and pour into a well-buttered 1½ qt. (1.5 L) shallow baking dish.

Bake in the oven for 2-2 ½ hours, stirring every 15 minutes during the first hour. After the first hour, pour cream over the top of the pudding and continue to bake without stirring in the cream.

Serve warm and top with fresh whipped cream, creme fraiche, or ice cream.

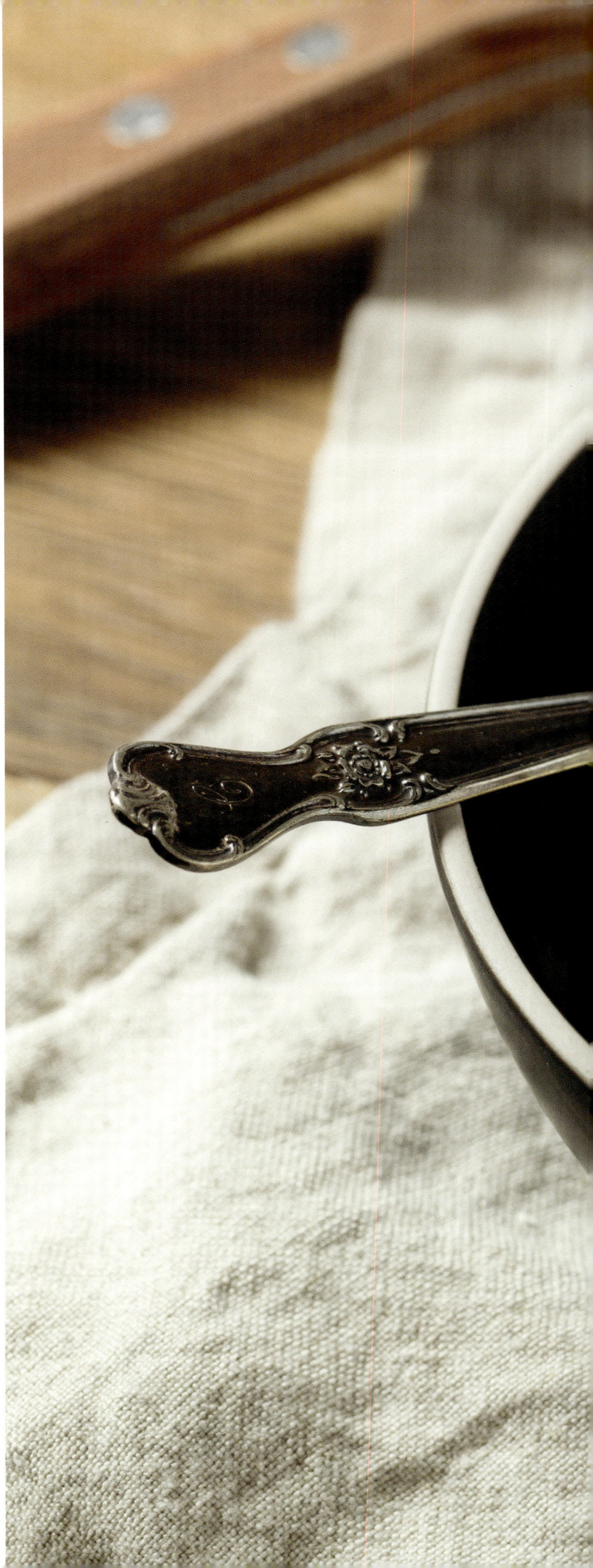

Southern American Cuisine

It is impossible to discuss traditional American cuisine without paying homage to the rich flavors and history that engulf its southern region. The Southern kitchen is truly a "melting pot" experience formed over 300-plus years, incorporating Native American, African, and European traditions. The South entices you with its perfect combination of sweet, savory, and spicy on one plate.

Southern folks in the United States LOVE their sweets and have created many international sensations: red velvet cake, pecan pie, banana pudding, and peach cobbler are only a few desserts birthed in the south.

In this book, I would like to share a southern American recipe that is very traditional but not widely known outside of the United States. It is a 7Up Cake (yes, made with real 7Up)! I remember my first experience with the cake via my grandma's friend Mother Griffin ("Mother" is a title given in most African American churches to senior female parishioners). Mother Griffin would come up from her home in the south every year to spend a month with my grandmother and even lead church revivals.

However, there was more to Mother Griffin's visits than purely religious activities. I always made an excuse during her visits to stay as long as I could at my grandparents' home. I knew the house would be filled with the aromas of some baked delight. Yeast rolls, cakes, pies! Mother Griffin would never disappoint; she always treated the family to something delicious each afternoon. I think her baked goods were always so tasty because she prepared them with 100 percent love and care. She was one of the sweetest ladies you would ever want to meet.

If you are from the South in the United States, this cake isn't strange to you. It takes the elements of a traditional pound cake to a completely new level! Mother Griffin died in her mid-90s. But she continues to live in the memories of the many people who were touched by her ministry and her kitchen. This one is for you, Mother Griffin.

MOTHER GRIFFIN'S 7UP CAKE

PREP	**COOK**	**SKILL LEVEL**	**SERVES**
20 mins.	90 mins.	Easy	8

INGREDIENTS

- **1½ cups unsalted butter, softened**
- **2½ cups granulated sugar**
- **5 large eggs, room temperature**
- **1 tsp. vanilla extract**
- **½ lemon, freshly squeezed**
- **½ lime, freshly squeezed**
- **zest of 1 lemon**
- **zest of 1 lime**
- **3 cups all-purpose flour, sifted**
- **½ tsp. salt**
- **¼ cup heavy whipping cream**
- **¾ cup 7Up soda**

Glaze:

- **1 cup of powdered sugar mixed with 2 tbsp. of 7Up**

INSTRUCTIONS

Preheat the oven to 325° F.

Generously grease and lightly flour a bundt pan. Set aside.

In a large bowl, cream butter, shortening and sugar.

Mix in the eggs one at a time.

Fold in the vanilla extract and lemon juice.

Fold in the lemon zest and lime zest.

Gradually add in the flour and salt, and mix until combined.

Mix in the heavy whipping cream and 7Up until well combined and the batter is fluffy.

Spoon batter into bundt pan.

Bake for 1 hour, then check it. Bake until a knife inserted into the middle comes out clean, possibly 10-15 minutes more.

Let the cake sit in the pan until it is warm to the touch.

Remove from pan and place on a cooling rack until completely cooled.

Drizzle with 7Up glaze if desired.

JEREMIAH KNIGHT

Thanksgiving

Thanksgiving is undoubtedly a centerpiece of American culinary traditions. This might explain why I love the holiday so much: Family and food are always a winning combination. I love to use Thanksgiving as an opportunity to break the stereotypical view that American food is just hamburgers and hotdogs. Growing up, my home was the center of Thanksgiving celebrations for my family. My mom would begin creating the feast at least three days in advance – marinating, chopping, and prepping. On Thanksgiving Day our home would be packed with relatives coming and going until late in the night, each one of them leaving with bellies full of laughter and savory sweet satisfaction.

Thanksgiving is probably the only time during the year when I adhere to strict rules when it comes to creating the menu. To me, it is culinary diplomacy at its best. Through each dish, I share my African American heritage from the deep south and the undeniable New England homestead. Other key elements are tossed in and wrapped up in this celebration of thankfulness and family.

Over the decades, carrot soufflé has found its way into Thanksgiving and Easter dinners throughout the United States. It was never a part of my family's holiday menus, but once I discovered it later, I became a big champion of it.

SAGE BUTTER CARROT SOUFFLÉ

PREP	COOK	SKILL LEVEL	SERVES
45 mins.	40 mins.	Medium	12

INGREDIENTS

- 2 lbs. carrots, peeled and diced
- ½ tsp. salt
- 4 tbsp. flour
- ½ tsp. ground cinnamon
- ½ tsp. ground nutmeg
- 1 tsp. baking powder
- ½ tsp. baking soda
- ¼ cup unsalted butter, melted
- 4-5 large leaves of fresh sage
- ½ cup brown sugar, firmly packed
- 3 large eggs
- ½ cup heavy cream
- 1 tsp. vanilla flavoring
- 1 tbsp. molasses
- 1 cup raisins
- powdered sugar for dusting

INSTRUCTIONS

Preheat oven to 350⁰ F.

Dice carrots and place in a medium saucepan to steam. Cook for 20-25 minutes or until very soft.

Once carrots are soft, drain. Add carrots to a food processor and blend until smooth. (Alternatively, mash them until well blended.)

Add all dry ingredients (including raisins and sugar) and blend.

In a separate saucepan, melt butter with sage leaves until leaves turn brown. Remove from heat and remove leaves from butter. Pour infused butter into carrot mixture.

Add heavy cream and vanilla flavoring to carrots mixture.

Whisk eggs until light and fluffy, then add to mixture.

Pour mixture into a buttered 9-inch round baking dish, or similar dish.

Bake for 40 minutes or until set and golden brown.

Before serving, dust with powdered sugar or add fresh whipped cream.

JEREMIAH KNIGHT

JEREMIAH'S THANKSGIVING TURKEY

PREP
3 days

COOK
2/2.5 hours

SKILL LEVEL
Medium-Hard

SERVES
10-12

INGREDIENTS

- one 14-15 lb. turkey
- 4 bottles white wine (preferably a Chardonnay or Sauvignon blanc)
- 1 bunch fresh parsley
- 1 bunch fresh rosemary
- 1 bunch fresh thyme
- 1 bunch fresh sage
- 5-6 cloves garlic
- 4 tbsp. sea salt (or Himalayan pink salt)
- 2 tbsp. coarsely ground white pepper
- 3 tsp. smoked paprika
- 1 large white onion
- 1 large sweet pepper
- 2 tsp. oregano
- 3 tbsp. olive oil
- 3 tsp. flour
- 1 oven roasting bag

INSTRUCTIONS

Fill the turkey's cavity with fresh herbs, garlic (sliced in half), onions (chopped in quarters), and sweet pepper (sliced in quarters).

Place turkey in an oven-roasting bag and pour in white wine along with 2 tablespoons of salt.

Place the turkey set in brine mixture in the refrigerator for 3 days (turn the turkey daily from one side to the other).

Remove the turkey from the brine and empty its cavity. Pour out brine but reserve the herbs, seasonings, onions, garlic, and sweet pepper.

Rub turkey inside and out with olive oil.

Season turkey inside and out with remaining salt, pepper, oregano and paprika.

Return herbs, onions, garlic, and sweet pepper to the cavity of the turkey.

Dust oven-roasting bag with flour and then place turkey inside.

Roast at a temperature of 350^{0} F for 2-2.5 hours.

Remove from the oven and carefully open the bag. Allow turkey to sit for one hour before removing it from the bag.

DOMINICAN REPUBLIC

Anyone who meets me soon learns the special place that the Dominican Republic holds within my heart. I can go on and on and on about the Dominican Republic; my friends, family and soul are there. It is a very special country to me and is the place I have lived the most, and visited the most outside of the United States! From the first time I lived there in 2004, through to my second stint living there in 2013 and until the present day, not a year has passed without my feet touching the soil of my second home. There are so many memories etched in my heart that center on this mystical island nation. And of course, food has played a vital part of creating these memories.

The island is large enough to have clear regional delicacies, incorporating foods from its various immigrant groups. There are key ingredients that can be found in many local dishes including: bitter orange, oregano, garlic, cilantro, culantro, chives and of course homemade sofrito (or sazón). But what makes the culinary experience there so great is that you are always invited into someone's home to eat! Dominicans love sharing meals. Even at lunch time, I remember how everyone in my team would bring in their lunch and share portions with everyone else around the table. I love this!

Cherished memories season my experience of what Dominican cuisine is all about: fine dining in the establishments of some of my closest chef friends, eating in the home of my beloved family nestled in the quaint town of Bonao, sitting by the sea enjoying the freshest offerings of the southern Caribbean Sea. Because of this, it is *extremely hard* to highlight one dish (or even a dozen!) that represents the totality of my love for the nation. But I will try my best not to disappoint my Dominican family and friends.

August 2006 will forever be chiseled into my memory. I had completed my first assignment there as a U.S. diplomat which meant I would have to leave the Dominican Republic for my next adventure. I had formed so many close relationships that made leaving one of the most difficult things for me. Week after week of *despedidas* (goodbye parties) had me in a crazy emotional state. Dominicans are full of laughter, extremely inviting, always ready for a party, and in love with food!

One party that stands out the most was thrown by a very close friend and neighbor, internationally known merengue artist Peña Suazo. He invited over 40 of my friends to his home where he served a candlelit dinner with the formalities of a 5-star restaurant. The dinner was based completely upon Dominican dishes that had captured my heart. *Pescado con Coco* (fish in coconut sauce) was the shining star for the night! Since that night, every time I return to the Dominican Republic, Peña Suazo's lovely wife prepares the same dinner I enjoyed in 2006 with *Pescado con Coco* as its centerpiece. Trust me, food tastes a lot better when it is being prepared while dancing and having a good time!

I would do an injustice to the Dominican Republic and all my friends and family there if I didn't include this dish as part of what speaks to me about my second home. So in honor of my friend Peña Suazo I share my guarded recipe with the world!

DOMINICAN PESCADO CON COCO

PREP
15-20 mins.

COOK
15-20 mins.

SKILL LEVEL
Medium

SERVES
8-10

INGREDIENTS

- 5 filets of fresh tilapia
- 4-5 tbsp. of coconut oil
- 1 cup flour
- 1 large onion, diced
- 1 sweet red pepper, diced
- 3 cloves garlic, chopped
- 1 bunch cilantro
- 2 bay leaves
- 2 tsp. paprika
- 1 tbsp. of adobo seasoning
- 1 tsp. black pepper
- sea salt to taste

Sauce:
- 2 cans coconut milk
- 1 medium tomato
- 1 clove garlic
- 4 tbsp. tomato paste

INSTRUCTIONS

Thinly slice onions and sweet peppers in long portions and finely chop the cilantro. In frying pan, saute onions, garlic, sweet peppers, bay leaves and cilantro with salt and black pepper to taste.

Remove from the pan and set aside.

Season fish with sea salt, Adobo, black pepper, and paprika. Lightly flour fish and then brown in a shallow frying pan with olive oil for no more than 2-3 minutes on each side. Add the onion mixture with cilantro on top of the fish.

Use a blender to combine coconut milk, tomato, tomato paste, and garlic.

Pour mixture into a saucepan and simmer for 10 minutes.

Pour mixture over fish and cook for 5-6 minutes

Chef's tip: When simmering the coconut sauce for the Pescado con Coco, do so without a lid. You want the mixture to thicken. Placing the lid on it will not allow the water to evaporate.

AREPITAS DE YUCA

PREP
15-20 mins.

COOK
15-20 mins.

SKILL LEVEL
Medium

SERVES
8-10

I will never forget the times I cooked with my helper, Maria. She showed me so many wonderful things about the Dominican kitchen that I will never forget. I actually 'stole' her sofrito recipe (and she 'stole' my salad dressing recipe)! We have been friends for 17 years and have never missed out on calling to check on each other.

Some of my most memorable times come from making the annual trek to my family's home in Bonao where we would have Christmas Eve dinner. The cooking, drinking, gift exchanges, meals and after parties were legendary!

My family certainly knows that if you want to make me happy during a meal, bring out a couple of arepitas de yuca! These fried cassava fritters always make my mouth water and in my opinion are a perfect companion to any main dish! The hint of aniseed catches your taste buds by surprise and provides depth and texture to this simple but very delightful dish. You can use them as an appetizer or have them as a side dish. At the end of the day, they just taste really good, and I am sure it will be a hit with family and friends.

INGREDIENTS

- **1 lb. yucca (cassava)**
- **½ tbsp. sea salt**
- **½ tsp. aniseed**
- **1 egg**
- **1 tsp. melted butter**
- **3 tbsp. evaporated milk**
- **¼ cup grated parmesan cheese (optional)**
- **1 cup vegetable oil for frying**

INSTRUCTIONS

Peel, wash, and finely grate the yuca in a large bowl.

Add into grated yucca the sugar, salt, and aniseed.

Mix and drain all excess water.

Beat egg until fluffy and add to mixture along with butter and evaporated milk.

Add parmesan cheese if desired.

Heat oil in a frying pan.

Use two tablespoons to shape the yuca mixture into oval balls.

Place balls into hot oil and fry until they are golden brown.

Set aside to drain on paper towels and serve warm.

Chef's tip: It is very important that you get fresh yucca! When you are purchasing them, crack them open first. If you see a bunch of black lines on the inside, then you know it is not good yuca. It is supposed to be nice and white inside and relatively easy to crack.

MEXICO

My first experience with Mexico was for the wedding of my Mexican sister Florencia. Our friendship, which has spanned the last 20 years, has always incorporated many hours in the kitchen sharing our cuisines via our unique cultural backgrounds. Florencia is one of the few people in my life whom I enjoy inviting into the kitchen. Her willingness and enthusiasm to learn new cooking techniques and explore other cultures are second to none. I also have learned a great deal from her about Mexican cuisine. I vividly remember one day when she was teaching me how to make a dish and in pure Jeremiah fashion, I began to *doctor it up* based on how I thought it should come out. She never said much during the process, but at the end she stated, "Well Jeremiah, this tastes excellent to be honest. However, it is not the actual dish because you have made it something different. But that is ok, it still is good." I laughed so hard and apologized. The fusion-and-flavor lover in me had taken it a step too far. Never again did I try to run the show when she was teaching me how to make something. But her loving attitude and easy-going nature make her a natural partner in the kitchen.

Florencia's wedding was something taken straight out of a telenovela (Spanish soap opera): a wedding ceremony in a small village church, reception in a rustic *hacienda* (the Spanish word for a large estate), and night skies lit with fireworks highlighting silhouettes of well-wishers dancing the night away. My first experience with the nation will always be ingrained in my soul. I can clearly remember the day I arrived at the hacienda after traveling for about 8 hours from the Dominican Republic. I was greeted with a margarita and invited to a pre-wedding celebration already under way. Apart from the exquisite offerings of *tacos*, *flautas*, *churros* and other traditional dishes, it was the guacamole that captured me. They made it in the same style that Florencia showed me many years before in my kitchen. Her version of guacamole (which she taught me was a salad rather than a dip) was an instant hit among my friends and has been shared and enjoyed many times.

Florencia, thanks for all the wonderful culinary moments, friendship, and being my big sister! This is in honor of you!

FLORENCIA-STYLE GUACAMOLE

PREP
10 mins.

COOK
0

SKILL LEVEL
Easy

SERVES
6

INGREDIENTS

- 6 ripe hass avocados
- 2 medium ripe heirloom tomatoes
- ½ of a white onion, chopped finely
- ½ bunch of cilantro
- 2 limes (juice)
- 1 tbsp. virgin olive oil
- sea salt to taste
- 1 small serrano or jalapeño pepper, deseeded and chopped finely
- queso fresco or French feta to crumble on top (optional, to taste)

INSTRUCTIONS

In a non-metallic bowl – glass or plastic only – use a plastic knife to cut avocados (avoid metal contact with the avocados as they start to oxidize and turn black). Cut avocados lengthwise four times and then into chunky squares. Place in a bowl along with the seed (as the seed keeps the avocados from oxidizing and your guacamole fresher).

Dice tomatoes and onion (into medium chunks) along with the hot peppers, then add to the mix.

Remove leaves of cilantro from stems. Chop them and add the leaves to the mixture.

Add the lime juice, olive oil, and sea salt.

Mix gently and serve as a side to your main dinner dish, tortilla chips or hot tortillas.

Chef's tip: Be very light-handed and only use a wooden spoon. You don't want to make the salad mushy. When serving, also use a wooden spoon. This helps to prevent *oxidation* (like apples, or in this case, avocados). It's still tasty, just not so pretty to look at.

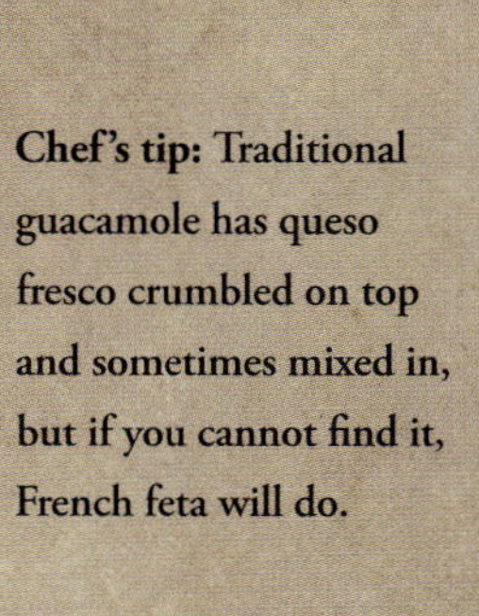

Chef's tip: Traditional guacamole has queso fresco crumbled on top and sometimes mixed in, but if you cannot find it, French feta will do.

MEXICAN SHRIMP COCKTAIL

PREP
3 hrs.

COOK
8 mins.

SKILL LEVEL
Easy

SERVES
8-10

This is a cold shrimp cocktail found commonly in the Northern Pacific region of Mexico where seafood is plentiful, and the hot weather demands a refreshing meal. It can be served as an appetizer or a meal with tortilla chips, tostadas, or plantain chips.

INGREDIENTS

- 2 lb. raw, tail-on shrimp
- 7 cups water
- 1 large English cucumber or two large regular cucumbers, peeled and diced
- 2 cups ripe beefsteak tomatoes (vine ripe or heirloom tomatoes will work too)
- 2 large jalapeños, diced
- ½ white onion, minced (can be substituted with a purple onion)
- ½ cup lime juice
- 2 tbsp. hot sauce (you can add more depending on your heat tolerance)
- 3 tbsp. tomato paste
- 2 cups shrimp broth from cooking the shrimp
- 1½ tsp. fine sea salt
- cilantro leaves for garnish

INSTRUCTIONS

Boil the 2 pounds of shrimp in the 7 cups of water for 5-8 minutes until the shrimp turns pink. Let the shrimp cool for 30 minutes before removing the tails. Keep two cups of the strained shrimp broth. Let the shrimp and the broth cool for at least 30 more minutes.

While shrimp and broth cool, dice cucumber, tomatoes and jalapenos, and mince onion.

Cut shrimp into ½ inch pieces, place in the bowl with the broth and mix in the diced and minced ingredients, along with the lime juice, hot sauce, tomato paste, and fine sea salt. Taste and adjust salt, hot sauce, and tomato paste as needed.

Garnish with cilantro leaves and place in the refrigerator for 2 hours to let the flavors mix.

Serve cold with tortilla chips, tostadas, or plantains.

JAMAICA

The way to a Jamaican's heart is to make some good home cooked food! Jamaicans unite over food like no other culture I have seen. They not only love their local food but are extremely (I say *extremely*) proud of it and welcome every opportunity to share it with the world! They are sticklers for traditional approaches too. It is hard to convince them to incorporate new views into it. And I don't blame them. Jamaican food to me is life!

Jamaican cuisine will always be dear to me. It was the first "non-American" style of cooking I learned. When I was 10 years old, I began cooking Jamaican food in the kitchen of my dear Aunt Megg (who emigrated from Jamaica many years before I was born). I often credit three individuals for my cooking skills: my mother (who showed me many culinary techniques), my grandma (who not only showed me how "soul" should be added into cooking but also allowed me space to fail), and my Aunt Megg (who opened my eyes to food beyond U.S. borders). My first international trip at age 12 was to Jamaica. I traveled with one of my brothers, my Aunt Megg, and my uncle to spend three weeks during the Christmas season with family. That trip forever changed my life, giving me a new perspective on part of my own culture and culinary traditions.

Though there isn't much in the line of "regional" cuisines on the island, what is offered is amazing. Because it has always been a part of my life, I couldn't imagine a world without it. This little island's "jerk" seasoning can be found literally all over the world. I clearly remember going into a market in Islamabad, Pakistan, and finding a bottle of Grace Jerk Seasoning! I was so astonished!

I have chosen not to include in this book the typical curry, jerk, or ackee. Instead, I have chosen to share three less globally celebrated recipes. These recipes remind me of my first experiences with Jamaican cuisine. When I partake, I think of my dear Aunt Megg and all she's taught me!

COCONUT TOTOS

PREP
15 mins.

COOK
40 mins.

SKILL LEVEL
Easy

SERVES
8-10

INGREDIENTS

- 3 cups all-purpose flour
- 1½ cups brown sugar
- 1½ cups grated coconut
- 3 tsp. baking powder
- 1 tsp. baking soda
- ½ tsp. allspice
- ½ tsp. nutmeg
- 1 tsp. freshly ground ginger
- ½ tsp. salt
- ½ cup golden raisins
- 2 eggs, well beaten
- 1½ cups milk
- ½ cup coconut milk
- ½ cup butter, melted
- 1 tsp. vanilla extract
- 1 tbsp. dark rum (optional)

INSTRUCTIONS

Preheat the oven to 350° F.

In a large bowl mix all dry ingredients.

Beat eggs and both types of milk together and add melted butter.

Add vanilla and rum (optional).

Add all liquid to bowl with dry ingredients and mix until blended. Do not over mix.

Place batter in a greased oblong baking dish (about 13" x 8") and bake for 1 hour.

Cool on rack in the baking dish and then cut into squares.

JAMAICAN SORREL

PREP
15-20 mins.

COOK
15-20 mins.

SKILL LEVEL
Medium

SERVES
8-10

Christmas isn't Christmas in Jamaica without sorrel. Sorrel is the unique way Jamaicans create a refreshing holiday drink out of the hibiscus flower. As a child, every year I looked forward to tasting my family's homemade sorrel. It was the perfect accompaniment to the warm, spicy flavors captured in Jamaican Christmas cake, curries and jerk dishes that fill homes during the holidays. The cold, short winter days of New England were transformed into tropical bliss upon entering the home of my Jamaican relatives.

Later on in life, during my travels throughout Latin America, the Caribbean, and Africa, I've tasted various versions of hibiscus-based drinks. My personal opinion is that all hibiscus drinks are refreshing, but Jamaicans have created the most unique approach to preparing this truly international drink. In keeping with tradition, I prepare sorrel every Christmas season and invite my friends to experience a taste of my childhood. Culinary traditions like these should be guarded to share with the next generation, just as I'm sharing this one with you!

INGREDIENTS

- 1 gallon of water
- 4-5 cups sorrel (dried hibiscus flower)
- the peel of one orange
- the peel of one lime
- 2-3 large pieces of ginger root
- 8 allspice berries
- 4 cloves
- 1½ cups brown sugar (or more to taste)
- 3-4 limes
- ¼ cup of white rum (optional)

INSTRUCTIONS

Roughly crush ginger and boil for 20 minutes with the peels, cloves and allspice.

Turn off heat and add sorrel, cover and let it sit overnight.

Strain and then add in brown sugar.

Finish with lime juice and white rum (optional).

Let the sorrel drink sit for at least one week before serving.

Chef's tip: The complex flavors of spices in sorrel taste even better when you let it sit for a while. By letting it age, the flavors become refined just as they would with a fine wine. I strongly suggest letting it sit in the refrigerator for at least a week before serving it. I have an aunt in Birmingham, England that lets it sit an entire year before sharing it with others!

JAMAICAN PICKLED SALTFISH

PREP
20 mins.

COOK
30 mins.

SKILL LEVEL
Medium

SERVES
8-10

This simple, but very tasty, pickled dish has somehow been missing from many menus of Jamaican restaurants and homes! It is a great "starter" dish that can be served with crackers or, if you happen to have roasted breadfruit, it can become a full meal.

INGREDIENTS

- 1 lb. salted codfish (boiled, deboned and shredded)
- ½ medium red onion
- 2 scallions
- ½ large red bell pepper
- ½ large yellow bell pepper
- 3 cherry tomatoes, de-seeded and diced
- ½ cup white vinegar
- 3 sprigs fresh thyme
- 1 lime (juice)
- 1 clove of garlic
- 2 tbsp. brown sugar
- 3-4 pimento berries (allspice seeds)
- ½ scotch bonnet pepper, de-seeded and chopped

INSTRUCTIONS

Rinse salted codfish and boil (changing the water at least twice) until it becomes tender. Shred and place aside in a bowl.

Chop scallions, and finely slice red onion, bell peppers and tomatoes. Place in the bowl with the codfish.

Crush and finely chop garlic along with scotch bonnet pepper, add them along with remaining ingredients (excluding the sugar, vinegar and lime juice) to the codfish.

Dilute sugar with vinegar and add to codfish, and then add lime juice.

Leave in the refrigerator for at least 3 hours.

Remove pimento berries and thyme sprigs.

Serve with crackers or preferably with roasted breadfruit.

THE BAHAMAS

Nassau, Bahamas, has to be one of the most beautiful tropical islands I have ever visited. Its clear blue waters and white sand beaches stretch from the downtown capital of Nassau to uninhabited cays located thousands of miles from humanity. I was invited to stay in Nassau for a week by a dear friend of mine who was working at the U.S. Embassy. Neda was the best host anyone could have in the Bahamas. She completely understood my passion for food and, having a paternal family from the island, provided me with a culinary journey from a local perspective. I definitely ate and drank my way through the island of New Providence which, is home to the nation's capital.

I was shocked to find grits and other African American dishes incorporated into Bahamian cuisine. But after being educated about the African American connection to the nation, it made sense. You see, around 1776, during the American Revolutionary War, Nassau was briefly held by the Americans. After the war, many loyalists, enslaved Black people, and freed men emigrated from the United States to the Bahamas. And of course they brought with them their cuisine.

The most memorable gastronomic moment occurred as a complete surprise for me. A day before departing the Bahamas, Neda drove me to her then 90-plus-year-old grandmother's home to say hello. To my surprise her grandmother presented me with two homemade Bahamian coconut tarts. The coconuts for these tarts came from her own backyard and were hand grated by her and her grandson. I packed them up in my luggage the next day and upon returning to the Dominican Republic, cut into my first slice. Right then I regretted not requesting two more! The simple and fresh ingredients, coupled with the delicate care of a woman who had been making them longer than I have been on earth, created a dessert I have ever-since craved. For about the next twelve days, I finished off my dinners with a thinly sliced serving of coconut tart, savoring each rationed piece. For this book, Neda has kindly shared her dear grandmother's recipe for everyone to enjoy!

Pay attention to your elders because you never know when they will leave you, silencing their secrets forever. Unfortunately, Neda's loving grandma passed away before this book was published. This recipe is in honor of her! Thanks, Grandma, for the memories and wonderful tasting coconut tart.

NEDA'S GRANDMA'S BAHAMIAN COCONUT TART

PREP
4 hours

COOK
40 mins.

SKILL LEVEL
Medium-Hard

SERVES
6

INGREDIENTS

Filling
- 3 cups freshly grated coconut
- 1 stick butter
- 2 tsp. vanilla flavoring
- 1 cup of brown sugar
- 1 cup of evaporated milk
- 1 tsp. nutmeg

Dough
- ¼ cup vegetable shortening
- ¼ cup butter
- 1 cup sugar
- 1 egg
- 1 teaspoon vanilla
- 1½ tsp. baking powder
- ¼ cup milk
- 2 ½ cups flour
- 3 tbsp. water

NORTH AMERICA & THE CARIBBEAN

INSTRUCTIONS

Begin by preparing the coconut filling, combining all ingredients in a saucepan over medium heat. Bring mixture to a boil and then reduce heat to simmer for 15-20 minutes or until the consistency becomes thick. Allow the mixture to cool.

For the dough, mix together shortening and butter until blended.

Mix together dry ingredients and begin adding the shortening-butter mixture little by little. Slightly knead dough.

Divide it into two equal portions, cover with plastic wrap and refrigerate for 1-2 hours. Roll out each to cover a 9"x9" pie dish.

Place one crust on the bottom of the dish and then fill with coconut filling. Cut the top cover into long strips and create a lace topping.

Add a dash of water to extra egg yolk and brush over the pie crust. Sprinkle with white granulated sugar if desired.

Bake at 350° F for about 40 minutes or until the crust is golden brown. Let cool for 15 minutes.

Chef's tip: This dish works best with freshly grated coconut. If you use dried coconut from the supermarket you need to increase the evaporated milk measurement to an additional cup to avoid dryness.

CONCH SALAD

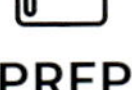

PREP
10 mins.

COOK
0

SKILL LEVEL
Easy

SERVES
3-4

During my first day in the Bahamas, I remember my friend Neda taking me to a small open-air restaurant near the ocean. The light ocean breeze, coupled with the smell of seafood being grilled, was intoxicating! After a welcome drink, she insisted that we start off with conch salad. She explained that it was one of the most traditional Bahamian dishes and I had to begin my culinary journey in the Bahamas with this salad. She was so right. This light, fresh salad has the right saltiness from the conch, coupled with the sweetness of the orange juice and spiciness of the hot peppers – a symphony of flavors which right away open your palate for more!

NORTH AMERICA & THE CARIBBEAN

INGREDIENTS

- 8 oz. cleaned conch, diced (canned if you can't get fresh ones)
- ¾ cup fresh lime juice
- ¼ cup fresh orange juice
- ½ cup diced tomato
- ¼ cup diced red onion
- 1 cucumber, peeled, seeded, and diced
- ½ medium sized bell pepper, diced
- 2 jalapeño peppers, minced
- salt and pepper, to taste

INSTRUCTIONS

Combine ingredients in a large bowl and mix thoroughly.

Cover and let marinate in the refrigerator for 1-2 hours.

Garnish with fresh cilantro if desired.

SOUTH AMERIC

CHILE | ARGENTINA | BRAZIL | ECUADOR | PERU | VENEZUELA

A

CHILE

When I was working as a consular officer, a little old lady came to my window for an interview. The first thing I noticed about her was how she presented herself: natural, well-dressed, inviting and elegant, yet unfussy. Consular interviews usually aren't the place people make friends or engage in chatty conversation, but this woman made my whole day. She not only smiled but seemed to be genuinely excited to talk to me. During the interview, I told her that she reminded me so much of my grandmother who was also very energetic. In response, she asked me *where in Africa did my grandmother live?* I was so tickled by her innocence! I gently corrected her, telling her my grandmother was American and did not live in Africa. She turned bright red with embarrassment, but I assured her that it was OK, and I wasn't offended by it.

I approved her visa and gave her instructions on how to receive the document in three days. She walked away and I began my next interview. A moment later she came back to my window, politely interrupting the start of my conversation. She explained that she couldn't wait three days; she was in a rush, already en route to her flight to see her granddaughter in New York. Some other people might get frantic in cases like these, but this sweet old lady's approach was something straight out of Diplomacy 101: she didn't yell, she didn't demand, and she certainly didn't demean when asking for what she wanted. She was so sweet in her approach that I did something that is almost unheard of – I printed the visa in her passport myself!

A month later, I had completely forgotten about our encounter. Then one afternoon the phone rang in my office. A voice stated, "Doña Juanita would like to talk to you." I was confused, still not knowing who this woman was. The next voice I heard was that of an old lady. She said, "Remember the crazy old lady that asked you if your grandmother lived in Africa?" We both laughed hard, happy for forgiveness and reunion, and we chatted for a bit. As fate would have it, through our conversation we realized that we lived only three blocks from each other. She invited me to *once*, the Chilean version of "teatime" normally held in the afternoon. The next day after work, I went directly over to her home and had *once* with Doña Juanita.

Over the years I became extremely close to Doña Juanita, and her family was just as gracious and welcoming. I learned that her deceased husband had been the head of Chilean Customs for many years, and we bonded over our world travels. Doña Juanita had a wonderful home on one of the famous hills of the ocean city of Valparaiso. She would often invite me to spend weekends with her family there. I remember celebrating birthdays, "New Year's", and summers with her. We had a standing appointment every week for *once* and even after I left Chile, we still talked almost every week. I shared a lot with her and learned a lot from her. She was indeed my Chilean grandmother, forever in my heart. (I spoke to my real grandmother at home about her; she smiled and was happy that another senior lady looked out for her grandson so well. The more love in the world the better!)

The one drink that most reminds me of Doña is the simple but refreshing *pisco sour*. She always had one ready when I visited. There is a long historic debate as to its origins (both Peruvians and Chileans place its origins in their homelands and claim it as their national drink). It is often hailed as Latin America's most elegant and classy cocktail, just as elegant and classy as Doña Juanita herself.

In recent years, Chileans have begun to experiment with adding exotic flavors of mango, summer berries, and cherries to their cocktails. However, I always come back to the classic version. Every time I drink a classic pisco sour I think of the times I spent on Doña Juanita's balcony with her family; pisco sour in hand, gazing out at the endless sea. Several years ago, my dear Doña Juanita passed away, but her memory lives with me forever!

CLASSIC PISCO SOUR

(with a twist!)

PREP
10 mins.

COOK
0

SKILL LEVEL
Easy

SERVES
2

INGREDIENTS

- 3 cups pisco
- 16 key limes, washed, deseeded, and cut in quarters
- simple syrup (to your liking)
- 1 egg white (optional)
- 2 drops Angostura bitters

SOUTH AMERICA

INSTRUCTIONS

In a blender, mix pisco and the key limes (4 at a time, allowing each batch to liquify).

Strain mixture. After all solid particles are removed, return liquid to a blender adding simple syrup mixture until you obtain desired sweetness.

Refrigerate until used.

When serving, whisk in egg whites (if desired) and top with bitters.

ENSALADA CHILENA

PREP
10 mins.

COOK
0

SKILL LEVEL
Easy

SERVES
6

Some of the best dishes I have found around the world are the ones presented in their natural state just as my Doña Juanita: well-dressed and inviting, yet not fussy. Somehow wonderfully simple and innocent.

Chilean salad is one of those dishes. During my years living in Santiago, I found this unassuming salad served with most typical traditional Chilean dishes. Due to its simple ingredients and subtle flavors, Chilean salad can accompany just about any meal you can imagine. It works best with grilled meats, but also can be used as an add-on to a vegetarian-inspired meal, or of course with Chilean corn casserole! I came to not only love this Chilean salad but eventually it found a home as a staple in my kitchen.

INGREDIENTS

- 5 large ripe tomatoes
- 1 large sweet yellow onion
- juice of ½ a lime
- 1 bunch of cilantro
- salt (to taste)
- fresh ground black pepper (to taste)
- ¼ cup virgin olive oil
- 3 tbsp. avocado oil
- a pinch garlic powder

INSTRUCTIONS

Cut onion in long thin slices and soak in warm water for 10 minutes.

Cut tomatoes in quarters, remove seeds (optional) and cut into medium slices.

Dice cilantro and set aside.

Remove onions from water and dry them with a paper towel.

Mix onions and tomatoes.

Add olive and avocado oil to mixture along with the juice of half a lime.

Add salt, pepper, and garlic powder and mix salad.

Add chopped cilantro.

Serve at room temperature and enjoy!

Chef's tip: I suggest never leaving a drop for the next day, just prepare what you can eat within one meal. Freshness is the key to capture the true essence of this ubiquitous Chilean dish.

SOUTH AMERICA

PASTEL DE CHOCLO

PREP
25-30 mins.

COOK
25 mins.

SKILL LEVEL
Medium

SERVES
8-10

Another dish that always brings me back to my time in Chile is *Pastel de Choclo*, a signature dish that captures the fresh artisanal spirit of the nation's gastronomy. My fondest memory of this delicacy was during my going-away lunch prepared by Rodrigo, the husband of my dear friend and colleague Ilsa. It was my last week in Chile, and Ilsa and her husband invited me to their home for a final goodbye. Rodrigo, of course knew of my love for *Pastel de Choclo* and decided to prepare a final one for me. His version was by far the best I had tried during my time in Chile. It was an unforgettable goodbye!

Pastel de Choclo highlights some of the best flavors Chile has to offer. A thick layer of fresh corn purée kissed with hints of basil atop a hearty surprise of meat accented with raisins, onions and oregano. After trying Rodrigo's version of the dish, I couldn't leave Chile without taking it with me! I share with the world Rodrigo's *Pastel de Choclo*!

INGREDIENTS

- 3 chicken breasts (whole) and 2 chicken thighs (deboned)
- 2 lbs. ground beef
- 12 ears of corn
- 3 large onions
- 3 cloves garlic
- ½ cup butter
- ¾ cup golden raisins
- ⅓ cup carnation milk
- 3-4 eggs
- 3 tbsp. brown sugar
- 3 tbsp. olive oil
- sea salt (to taste)
- black pepper (to taste)
- ¼ cup yellow cornmeal
- 3 tsp. cumin
- 1 tsp. oregano
- 2½ tsp. of paprika
- ¼ cup of fresh basil

INSTRUCTIONS

Preheat oven to 375^0 degrees F.

Dice the onions and sauté them with olive oil, black pepper, cumin, paprika, basil and oregano until they become translucent. Then add in diced chicken and cook until half cooked. Add in raisins and reserve aside. Saute ground beef and add to chicken mixture.

Grate the 12 ears of corn and then mix in a food processor. While blending add to the corn mixture, butter, basil, cornmeal, milk and sea salt. Cook on the stove at medium heat until it thickens. Place mixture aside and reserve in a separate container.

Boil the eggs. Peel, slice, and reserve.

Put the chicken/Beef mixture with onions and raisins in a large baking dish. Layer the sliced eggs on top.

Cover with the corn puree and lightly sprinkle brown sugar on top.

Bake it until golden brown.

Chef's tip: Fresh corn makes for the perfect *Pastel de Choclo*. If fresh corn on the cob isn't available, go with frozen corn over canned corn. You'll know the *Pastel de Choclo* is done when it has a nice golden-brown topping that is bubbling from the puréed corn and brown sugar. Let it cool for at least 20 minutes before serving; you don't want to burn your tongue; trust me, you'll want every taste bud to enjoy this!

JEREMIAH KNIGHT

ARGENTINA

Argentina is one of my favorite nations in South America. Walking on the streets of Buenos Aires gives you the feeling that you have been transported to an Italian city. (And yes, the Italian cuisine in Argentina is completely phenomenal!)

Yes, Argentineans speak Spanish, but the vibes there are very different from many other Latin American countries. I will never forget my very first trip to Argentina; I traveled with my dear friend Jessica. We both love to dance and so we had it in our minds to party the nights away. Buenos Aires is known to have a great nightlife scene. However, as fate would have it, we ate so much at one restaurant that *we couldn't fathom how we would make it back to the apartment*. The food was just that amazing!

One of the dishes I found myself ordering no matter what restaurant I went to was *provoleta*. A grilled piece of provolone cheese, topped with spices and a drizzle of olive oil, and accompanied with fresh bread, was the perfect way to begin any meal. Or course I had to try making it when I returned home.

The key to perfection with this simple dish is the *quality and thickness* of the cheese. You can top it with whatever you like, but I like to keep it traditional with a little kick!

PROVOLETA

PREP
10 mins.

COOK
2-3 mins.

SKILL LEVEL
Easy

SERVES
8-10

INGREDIENTS

- 2 wheels provolone cheese with peel (8-9 oz. each)
- 4 tbsp. extra virgin olive oil (or a bit more depending on your preference)
- 2 tsp. fresh oregano (or whole leaf dry oregano)
- sea salt or kosher salt (to taste)
- 1 tsp. crushed red-hot pepper
- 1 tbsp. flour

Chef's tip: To be honest, it is best to do provoleta on a grill. If you do not have access to a grill, I would say use an oven. To get that smoky flavor, brush it with a few drops of liquid smoke (found at most grocery stores) before flouring it.

SOUTH AMERICA

INSTRUCTIONS

Prepare the grill or oven. If you're using the oven, preheat to 325° F.

Place the wheels of cheese on a cookie sheet (if cooking in the oven). Dust both sides with flour and cover both sides with olive oil.

Sprinkle the oregano and crushed peppers on top of the cheese.

Place them on the grill or in the oven. Roast until each side has browned and they are soft without falling apart (about 2-3 minutes).

Add salt as needed and serve hot with fresh bread and chimichurri.

CHIMICHURRI SAUCE

PREP
10 mins.

COOK
0

SKILL LEVEL
EASY

SERVES
8-10

SOUTH AMERICA

When I lived in Chile, I would often take long weekend trips over to Argentina whenever I could. Once I went with a couple of friends on a scenic bus drive through the Andes Mountains to explore the town of Mendoza, famous for its wines and olive oil. Each night we planned to party after dinner but, just as it was on my first trip with my friend Jessica, our blissfully stuffed bellies cemented us to our hotel beds after each evening meal. Argentina is the only country that has ever consistently canceled my plans with nightly food comas!

Argentineans are avid meat lovers. As is the case in most countries located in South America, beef is king. Argentina is renowned for its beef barbeque (*asados*). I don't eat red meat, so I was unable to certify just how good it is. It was funny to see the faces of those who worked in restaurants when I ordered chicken and other non-red-meat dishes. I would often be encouraged to just have a try and my refusal confused them! Although I don't eat red meat, I was enchanted by the *chimichurri* sauce that always accompanied the grilled meat. This flavorful sauce somehow enhances the richness of meat (whether it is beef or chicken) without overpowering it or changing its flavor. I adopted this sauce as a staple in my kitchen for whenever I break out a grilled meat number from my repertoire. Fresh condiments provide an additional chorus line for a dish that has already soloed so well.

INGREDIENTS

- ½ cup olive oil
- 2 tbsp. red wine vinegar
- ½ cup finely chopped parsley
- 3-4 cloves garlic, crushed and chopped
- 2-3 scallions, chopped
- 1 red chili, deseeded and finely chopped
- 3 tbsp. finely chopped fresh oregano
- 2 tsp. fresh lime juice
- sea salt and crushed black pepper to taste
- ⅓ cup fresh chives

INSTRUCTIONS

Mix all ingredients together in a bowl and let it rest for at least 1 hour before serving.

The sauce can be refrigerated but must be used within 1-2 days.

Chef's tip: Depending on my mood, I sometimes substitute all of the vinegar with a mixture of lemon and lime juice. I find this flavor complements poultry and fish better; vinegar (in my opinion) better complements hearty meats. Also, be free with the fresh herbs to make it your own. You don't have to use only the ones I've mentioned. For instance, although not traditional, marjoram is a nice addition to this recipe. Its light, sweet, and woodsy characters add a new dimension of flavor to the chimichurri.

BRAZIL

Euphoria is the first word that comes to mind to describe the feelings associated with the ocean breezy air, the rainbow of vibrant people, and the overall allure of Brazil. The bustling big city vibes of São Paulo provided the perfect opportunity for me to explore the country's unexpected flavors, including its well-known Japanese-Brazilian cuisine. And of course, Rio de Janeiro!

Besides Brazil's scenic beaches, ocean views, and the tapestry of mountains, what it offers for the palate is second to none. The crisp flavors of fresh *caipirinhas* (Brazil's national cocktail) and the scent of grilled meat kept my mouth watering during my first time visiting this magnificent country.

I fondly remember when I visited my friend Carmelia for *Semana Santa*, the Holy Week leading up to Easter. I was in a little bit of a slump at the time. Being around a vibrant culture and having amazing food was the comforting respite and recharge I needed. Everyone needs that once in a while. That is why I always advise people to pick countries that will cause both the spirit and stomach to be recharged. I'm the type of person who receives energy from the good vibes of others. I live for it. I am an eternally optimistic and overall happy person. I have been to some amazing places that were aesthetically beautiful, but the interactions with the locals (and experience with their food) were lackluster. I personally would rather go to a hidden gem that may not have all the amenities in the world, but where the vibes of the people and the soul in the food bring me life!

There was one simple delicacy that I indulged in endlessly while spending *Semana Santa* in Brazil: *Pão de queijo*, humble yet remarkable cheese bread. It not only caught my attention but had me searching daily for it as I explored the country. One day while living in the Dominican Republic, my Brazilian soul sister Priscilla surprised me with a batch of *Pão de queijo* and it transported me back to my stay in her beautiful country. Thank you Priscilla for sharing this recipe of yours with me and the world!

PRISCILLA'S PÃO DE QUEIJO

PREP
25 mins.

COOK
25 mins.

SKILL LEVEL
Medium

SERVES
10-15

INGREDIENTS

- 4 cups tapioca flour
- 1 tbsp. salt
- 2 cups whole milk
- 1 cup canola oil
- 3 eggs
- 4 cups shredded semi-cured cheese (you can substitute with parmesan cheese or any other hard gratable cheese)
- ¼ cup chives (optional)

SOUTH AMERICA

INSTRUCTIONS

Preheat the oven to 375º F.

Pour oil, milk, and salt into a large saucepan, and place over high heat. When the mixture comes to a boil, remove from heat immediately, and stir in tapioca flour and chives until smooth. Set aside to rest for 10-15 minutes.

Stir the cheese and eggs into the tapioca mixture until well combined. The mixture will be chunky like cottage cheese. Drop rounded, ¼ cup-sized balls of the mixture onto an ungreased baking sheet.

Bake in a preheated oven until the tops are lightly browned, 15-20 minutes.

Chef's tip: The bread has to be rolled small. Do not make the pieces large. It will affect how they bake and also their texture. I like to brush them with a little melted butter right when taken out of the oven and sprinkle with some additional cheese.

COUVE A MINEIRA

PREP
10 mins.

COOK
5 mins.

SKILL LEVEL
Easy

SERVES
6-8

SOUTH AMERICA

I remember upon arriving in Rio that I wanted to make sure I had the opportunity to experience Afro-Brazilian cuisine. I had already been exposed to the Japanese-Brazilian fusion; however, I wanted to see the food linkages between the Afro-Brazilian palate and those found in Caribbean and African American cuisine: Black beans, coconut, plantain, hearty stews with okra, collard greens and hot peppers are a few items from the Afro-Brazilian kitchen that made me feel right at home.

Anyone who has tried African American cuisine understands how important collard greens are to the soul of "Soul Food." During my travels in Brazil I was amazed to find that Brazilians also love collard greens! It doesn't matter where you come from in the African diaspora, our kitchens are united!

Unlike the American version which has hearty flavors of smoked or salted meat and several spices, the finely sliced Brazilian version relies on only a few elements for a more salad-type interpretation. I played around a bit with this recipe, incorporating elements of the African American version to the base of its Brazilian counterpart. Enjoy!

INGREDIENTS

- **3 bunches collard greens (you can substitute with kale)**
- **4-6 cloves garlic**
- **sea salt to taste**
- **1½ - 2 tbsp. coconut oil**
- **2 shallots**
- **1 bay leaf**
- **½ tsp. fresh ground black pepper**
- **½ tsp. crushed red pepper flakes**
- **½ a lime**
- **¼ cup chopped bacon (optional and use turkey bacon if you do not eat pork)**

INSTRUCTIONS

Wash the collard greens well. Remove the majority of the stems and then gather bunches of the leaves together, roll them, and cut them into very thin strips.

If you are using bacon in the recipe, cook 3-4 pieces of bacon until crispy, chop and reserve.

Mash the garlic with the sea salt with a mortar and pestle.

Using the same skillet in which you cooked the bacon, heat the coconut oil over medium heat. Add in bay leaf for 1 minute or so. Add garlic and salt mixture, and cook, stirring until the mixture turns a golden color. Add in diced shallots.

Add the greens and sauté 3 or 4 minutes until they are bright green and start to soften.

Remove the bay leaf. Add black pepper, red pepper flakes, and additional salt (if needed).

Finish off with a squeeze of fresh lime and chopped bacon.

Chef's tip: You can substitute bacon with a nice piece of finely diced ham or even turkey ham, but whatever you do, DO NOT OVERCOOK YOUR GREENS! This is a collard green "salad" not traditional collard greens done American style. They need to be bright vibrant green and not a dark color. This is why it is so important to cut them super thin. When you cut them thin, they cook a lot faster.

ECUADOR

I was only in Ecuador for about four days for work; and most of that time I was trying to manage my altitude sickness! The capital city of Quito is extremely high and the altitude's effect on newcomers can be unrelenting at times. However, it's all worth it when you begin to explore the rich culinary offerings of this nation. I was really impressed with the presentation, variety, and the flavors I experienced in Ecuador. It didn't matter if I went to a fancy establishment or a small family-owned one, the detail and care were amazing. I had not been exposed to Ecuadorian food prior to my trip there and had no expectations; so it was a delightful surprise!

The nation's majestic marine life offers some of the best seafood delights in the world. I remember the first time I tried Ecuadorian-style shrimp ceviche. After years of living in South America, I thought I had experienced it all when it came to ceviche. Boy, was I wrong! The Ecuadorian version captivated me the entire time I was there. It seemed like each day I found myself ordering it! Upon my return home, I fooled around with some Ecuadorian shrimp ceviche recipes, incorporating the warm spices of the Caribbean until I created a balanced fusion of flavors. I hope you enjoy my ode to this classic Ecuadorian dish.

ECUADORIAN SHRIMP CEVICHE

PREP
30 mins.

COOK
0

SKILL LEVEL
Easy

SERVES
6-8

INGREDIENTS

- 2 lb. fresh large shrimp
- 2 red onions, sliced very thinly
- 4 large tomatoes
- the juice of 10-15 limes
- the juice of 1 bitter orange or a ruby red grapefruit
- 1 bunch cilantro
- sea salt (to taste)
- freshly ground white pepper (to taste)
- 3-4 tbsp. olive oil

SOUTH AMERICA

INSTRUCTIONS

Soak the onion slices in the lime and bitter orange juices with sea salt while preparing other parts of the recipe (about an hour before).

Blend two large tomatoes and set aside.

Dice remaining tomatoes and set aside.

Finely chop cilantro and set aside.

Clean and rinse large shrimp. Place in a large bowl and then add all other ingredients except cilantro.

Let the mixture sit for 15-20 minutes or until raw shrimp turns pink.

Add chopped cilantro and then serve.

Chef's tip: Remember, not every dish is "cooked" with heat. The key to this dish is not to let it sit for too long. I have seen a number of ceviche recipes that require you to let it sit for hours, or even leave the dish overnight and serve it the next day. DO NOT DO THAT! The acid from the lime will overcook the shrimp if left that long.

PERU

I flew from Santiago, Chile, to the Chilean border town of Arica where I spent about three days on a work assignment. During that time, I decided to take the 21-mile trip across the border to visit Tacna, Peru. The couple of hours I spent in this quaint border town were unforgettable. The vibrancy of the people, art, and cuisine were incomparable. One of the things I loved the most was that you didn't have to spend a fortune to eat and drink well. Pisco sours are served in large quantities, fresh ceviche is on every corner, and the numerous markets intoxicate your soul! Right away I decided that I had to revisit Peru and get to know the nation better. Fried green plantain, river ceviche, mangos, and other tropical flavors made me feel right at home!

During my second trip to Peru I visited the nation's capital of Lima. It was there that my friend Irene (who was serving as secretary to the U.S. Ambassador to Peru) invited me to dinner. She was Peruvian by birth and decided to take me to one of the most elegant restaurants in the country. I remember her telling me that I could not leave Peru without trying *aji de gallina*, a spicy creamy chicken dish that she paired with the perfect white wine.

She was 100% correct, it would have been a culinary sin to leave the country and not taste this signature Peruvian dish. Every time I make *aji de gallina* I think of the wonderful evening I had with my dear friend Irene. She has since retired from the U.S. Foreign Service.

Irene, this recipe is in your honor and in appreciation of your friendship!

AJI DE GALLINA

PREP
30-35 mins.

COOK
1 hr.

SKILL LEVEL
Advanced

SERVES
4

INGREDIENTS

- 1 complete chicken breast (both halves)
- 2 large slices of a baguette (or 1 packet of soda crackers)
- 1 yellow onion, chopped
- 4 cloves of garlic, crushed and chopped
- 1 tsp. fresh oregano (or ½ tsp. dried oregano)
- 3 tbsp. ground yellow chili pepper (or 2 whole yellow chilies)
- ½ cup evaporated milk
- 3 yellow potatoes, boiled (yellow)
- 5 black olives
- 3 boiled eggs
- 1 bay leaf
- 1 tsp. cumin
- ¼ cup olive oil
- ½ cup grated parmesan cheese
- salt (to taste)
- white pepper (to taste)

SOUTH AMERICA

INSTRUCTIONS

In a heavy saucepan, cook the chicken breast in water with salt, pepper and the bay leaf for 15-20 minutes.

Shred the meat with two forks or with your fingers and reserve. Strain and reserve the stock. Place bread slices in a bowl and add one cup of the stock. When the bread has absorbed the stock, process in a blender to form a loose paste. Reserve.

In the same saucepan you used, heat the oil and sauté fresh oregano, onion, and garlic for 8-10 minutes or until translucent. Add yellow chili pepper and continue to cook for about 5 minutes.

Add the bread mixture with an additional cup of chicken stock. Cook and stir until mixture starts to thicken.

Add shredded chicken with cheese. Season with salt and pepper to taste.

Add evaporated milk, stir and turn off the heat. If it looks too thick, thin it with more chicken stock.

Cut the cooked potatoes in thick slices and put 2 pieces on every plate. Cover with the Aji de Gallina and serve with white rice.

Decorate with black olives and hard-boiled eggs cut in halves or quarters.

Chef's tip: Make sure that when you are preparing the *Aji de gallina*, the consistency is rich and thick. If it is too watery you can add a little bit more cheese. It should be creamy and a nice yellow color.

LOMO SALTEADO

PREP
15 mins.

COOK
10 mins.

SKILL LEVEL
Easy

SERVES
2

INGREDIENTS

- 1 lb. sirloin steak cut in thin slices
- salt and pepper
- 3 tbsp olive oil
- 2 cloves of garlic (crushed)
- 1 red onion cut in thick slices
- 2 tomatoes cut in thick slices
- 1 tbsp. of chili pepper paste or one fresh chili cut very thin (leave seeds in for extra heat if desired)
- 3 tbsp. soy sauce
- 3 tbsp. red wine vinegar
- 1 tbsp. brown sugar
- 1 tsp. cornstarch
- ½ cup fresh cilantro, chopped
- 2 cups French fries and white rice as a side dishes

SOUTH AMERICA

INSTRUCTIONS

Season the sirloin steak with salt and pepper.

Put a wok or a pan over very high heat. Add the oil and saute the meat, a few slices at a time so they don't steam for about 10-12 mins.

Add the garlic, onion, tomato, chili pepper, and stir for a couple of minutes.

Add the soy sauce and vinegar to the sides of the pan and mix everything. Season with more salt and pepper and the brown sugar.

Lower heat and add in cornstarch (mix the cornstarch with 2 tbsp of water first, then pour in). Cook for an additional 5 mins.

Take off the heat, add chopped cilantro and serve at once with French fries and white rice.

JEREMIAH KNIGHT

VENEZUELA

So I thought I knew what *arepas* were all about until I rediscovered them in Caracas, Venezuela. You see, Venezuela is familiar with Caribbean cuisine; it's just a ferry ride away from Trinidad and Tobago. Caribbean influence is most definitely felt in Venezuela music, folkloric traditions and of course its cuisine. Because of this, Venezuela and several Caribbean islands share similar ingredients, flavors, and even names of foods, but their cuisines are still prepared in distinct ways. From Venezuela hearty stews, healthy servings of black beans and rice, to *polvorosa de pollo* (the nation's response to a chicken pot pie), the culinary story of Venezuela is interpreted through its unique mixture of Indigenous populations and a variety of immigrants who all make it what it is today. One dish that embodies this is the Venezuelan *arepa*.

My very first morning waking in the mountains of Caracas, I walked into my friend Florencia's kitchen where I found interesting-looking *arepas* on my plate. After living in the Dominican Republic, my version of a morning *arepa* would be that of a sweet, dense cornmeal cake speckled with raisins, and almost always served with hot chocolate. However, this was not the case in Venezuela. This nation's *arepa* is round, cut almost in half, and filled with a number of breakfast items including cheese and eggs and served with fresh juice and a cup of rich dark coffee.

Throughout my week in Venezuela I sampled various versions of the nation's *arepa* but always seemed to go back to the one I am sharing with you in this book. What makes me love this one the most is its filling. As a lover of avocados and everything to do with them, I became an instant fan of this creamy chicken and avocado based filling. The credit for this recipe goes directly to a wonderful Venezuelan chef who happens to be my friend! Wendy, thanks for not only sharing your recipe with me, but also with the world!

AREPAS VENEZOLANAS CON RELLENO REINA PEPIADA

PREP
20 mins.

COOK
20 mins.

SKILL LEVEL
Advanced

SERVES
4

INGREDIENTS

Dough:

- 2 cups pre-cooked cornmeal bread flour
- 3 ½ cups water
- 2 pinches salt
- 1 egg

Filling:

- 1 chicken breast (preferably roasted chicken)
- 2 small avocados or 1 large one that is mature but not overripe
- 1 cup plain yogurt without sugar or mayonnaise
- 1 bunch cilantro
- salt and pepper (to taste)
- 3 tbsp. mustard
- 1 white onion or medium red
- 1 red pepper

Chef's tip: Though there are only a few ingredients that go into making *arepas*, the success in making a great one comes from trial and error. Do not overwork the dough in your hands. Let it rest a little before you place it to cook on top of the stove.

SOUTH AMERICA

INSTRUCTIONS

Dough:

Mix the water with the salt in a bowl and add the flour. Knead by hand until you are able to make a smooth ball that will remain together with no lumps.

Add egg and re-knead.

Create palm-sized flat dough circles.

Heat oil in a cast-iron pan. Once oil is nice and hot, place dough in and then lower flame.

Cook until golden brown on each side.

Remove from heat and allow to cool.

Filling:

In a bowl mix yogurt and mustard.

Chop onion and sweet pepper in small squares, finely chop cilantro and reserve each individually.

Heat a frying pan with a touch of butter or olive oil. When this is hot, add the onion, let it brown a little, then the aji leaves, and then the chicken for about 5 minutes.

Remove from the heat and let it cool a little.

In a large bowl, add chicken mixture, the yogurt mustard mixture and then a touch of salt and pepper if necessary.

Finish by adding the avocado, crushing with a fork and incorporating everything evenly.

As a final touch, add chopped cilantro.

Serve the *arepas* and the stuffing separately so they can be filled at the table – Mmmmm divine.

Chef's tip: If you do not have roasted chicken then take a raw breast and put it in a pot to cook with onion, garlic and aji gustoso and then perform the process described in the instructions. When filling the *arepa*, to ensure that the filling will be contained, do not fully open it. Just make a pocket with a knife.

VENEZUELAN PERICO

PREP
5 mins.

COOK
10 mins.

SKILL LEVEL
Easy

SERVES
6

SOUTH AMERICA

INGREDIENTS

- 9 eggs
- 2 tbsp. olive oil
- 1 yellow onion, finely chopped
- 4 medium or 6 small ripe tomatoes, chopped
- coarse sea salt
- black pepper (to taste)
- ¼ cup cilantro leaves (reserve some for garnish)

INSTRUCTIONS

Sauté onion with olive oil on medium heat until it becomes translucent.

Add the tomatoes, black pepper and cilantro and cook for about 5 minutes at a lower heat. Turn up heat and add eggs. Cook uncovered for about 3 minutes, stirring continuously.

Add salt to taste and garnish with remaining cilantro.

Serve warm with Arepas.

APPENDIX A

FOOD ALPHABETIZED IN CATEGORIES

Salads

Starters

Side Dishes

Main Course

Sauces & Spices

Desserts

Drinks

APPENDIX B

ALL FOOD ALPHABETIZED

APPENDIX B